THE BASICS OF

ATOMS AND MOLECULES

CORE CONCEPTS

THE BASICS OF

ATOMS AND MOLECULES

ANNE O'DALY

ROSEN PUBLISHING

Published in 2024 by The Rosen Publishing Group, Inc.
2544 Clinton Street, Buffalo, NY 14224

First edition published 2014. Second edition 2024.

Editor: Lindsey Lowe
Children's Publisher: Anne O'Daly
Design Manager: Keith Davis
Designer: John Woolford
Picture Manager: Sophie Mortimer
Consultant: Adrian Dingle

Cataloging-in-Publication Data

Names: O'Daly, Anne, 1966-.
Title: The basics of atoms and molecules / Anne O'Daly.
Description: Second edition. | New York : Rosen Young Adult, 2024. | Series: Core concepts | Includes glossary and index.
Identifiers: ISBN 9781499475500 (pbk.) | ISBN 9781499475517 (library bound) | ISBN 9781499475524 (ebook)
Subjects: LCSH: Nuclear physics--Juvenile literature. | Atomic theory--Juvenile literature. | Matter--Properties--Juvenile literature. | Molecules--Juvenile literature.
Classification: LCC QC778.5 O34 2024 | DDC 539.7--dc23

Manufactured in the United States of America

CPSIA Compliance Information: Batch #CW24RYA. For further information, contact Rosen Publishing, New York, New York, at 1-800-237-9932.

CONTENTS

CHAPTER 1

What Is Matter?

Matter is the material from which Earth and the universe are made. There are three main states of matter: solid, liquid, and gas. All matter is made from tiny particles called atoms. Chemistry studies the properties and behaviors of matter.

Everything in the universe is made from matter. Matter is anything that has mass and takes up space (has volume). Matter is made up of tiny building blocks called atoms. Chemistry is the science that investigates how atoms are organized to make the substances around us. Everything around you is made of matter. The pages of this book, the air you breathe, and even your body are made from the same building blocks. They do not make up just the things on Earth. Everything in the universe—the sun, billions of other stars, rocks, and dust—are made of the same building blocks.

What Are Atoms?

The building blocks of matter are called atoms. Atoms are far too small to see with the naked eye. About 125 million atoms lined up in a single row would be 1 inch (2.5 cm) long. Not all atoms are the same. There are about 90 different types in nature. Atoms come in different sizes and masses and have many properties. Small groups of atoms that are bonded together are called molecules.

← Elements are formed by the stars. As stars burn, they create new elements. When a star explodes as a supernova, these new elements are flung out into space. This picture is an artist's impression of a supernova exploding somewhere in the universe.

DENSITY

One of the main properties of matter is density. Density is a measure of how much matter a substance has packed inside it. Density is measured by comparing an object's mass with its volume. Certain materials contain a lot of large, heavy atoms or have molecules packed closely together. This arrangement makes even small volumes of such materials very heavy. Scientists describe these substances as having a high density. For example, lead is an extremely dense metal. It is used to make weights. Other substances have small atoms that are spread out. Helium gas is one of the least dense substances known to science. It is used inside airships to make them light enough to float in the air.

Airships are filled with helium to make them lighter than air. In the past, hydrogen was used to fill airships, but hydrogen is very flammable. Its use led to a number of airships being destroyed by fire, killing the passengers. Although helium is heavier than hydrogen, it is non-flammable and therefore safer.

Atoms group together to make the objects and other materials around us. Matter that contains just one type of atom is called an element. For example, a gold nugget contains only gold atoms. Other elements include carbon, iron, aluminum, sulfur, and oxygen.

Compounds and Molecules

Elements are unique materials because they cannot be broken up into simpler ingredients. However, not everything in the universe is made of pure elements. Most things contain combinations of the atoms of several different elements. Various combinations of different types of atoms are called compounds. When the atoms group together, they make a structure called a molecule. A molecule has a unique shape and size. This gives a material certain properties, such as making it hard or bendable.

Compounds frequently have properties that are different than those of the elements included in the molecule. For example, as an element, sodium is a soft metal that reacts violently with water. Chlorine is a highly reactive gas. When combined as the compound sodium chloride, sodium and chlorine form a glassy crystal that is stable, safe, and unreactive at room temperature. We know it as table salt.

Solid, Liquid, or Gas?

All matter has three basic forms, or states: solid, liquid, and gas. There is a fourth state of matter, called plasma, but most of the material on Earth tends to exist as a solid, a liquid, or a gas. A solid, such as stone, is hard and has a fixed shape. A liquid, such as water, takes on the shape of its container. It can flow from one shape into another, such as when it is poured into a new holder or pumped through a pipe. In this respect, a gas is similar to a liquid because it, too, takes on the shape of its container. However, liquids always sit at the bottom of a container. Gases are different. They fill all the available space by spreading out so that their atoms or molecules are evenly dispersed

KEY TERMS

Atom: The smallest independent building block of matter.
Element: A material that cannot be broken up into simpler ingredients.
Molecule: Two or more connected atoms that have a unique shape and size.

Erupting volcanoes show matter in all three states—the solid rock that forms the volcano, the liquid magma that pours out of it, and the gases that are blasted into the atmosphere.

ICE, WATER, STEAM

Volume is the measurement of the amount of space a substance occupies. So does volume change with the state of matter? Take an empty ice cube tray and fill the compartments with water. Put the tray in the freezer until the water is frozen.

Now leave the tray in a warm spot indoors. After awhile, the ice will have melted into water. Has any water spilled over into other compartments?

If you have been careful, no water should have spilled. Liquids have more or less the same volume as their solid states. Water is an unusual liquid because it expands slightly when it freezes. However, when the ice melts, the water should still all fit in its single compartment.

Now put the tray outside in a sunny place. After a few hours, most of the water will have evaporated into water vapor—it has become a gas. Gases *do* expand when they form and the molecules move farther apart.

This experiment demonstrates that molecules are more or less as tightly packed in a solid as they are in a liquid. However, in a gas, they are free to spread out completely.

throughout the entire container. In normal conditions, such as those found inside a house, each material will be in a certain state. Some are solids, such as metals and plastics. Some are liquids, such as water or fruit juice. Others are gases, such as the air. The state of each material depends on how its atoms and molecules are arranged.

In most solids, the particles (which can be atoms or molecules) are held in a rigid pattern called a crystal. The particles are arranged in a precise order that repeats throughout the crystal. This regular arrangement of the particles is what gives a solid its fixed shape. However, the particles that make up a substance are not motionless. They are always moving. Each particle vibrates inside the crystal, but it cannot move far because it is held in place by all the other particles around it. The heat given off by a solid is a measure of how much its atoms are moving around.

In some solids, the particles are not held in rigid patterns but are arranged in an

A diamond is a crystalline form of carbon. Its atoms are held in a rigid pattern. It is this structure that allows a diamond to be cut and polished into a sparkling gemstone.

irregular way. These solids are called amorphous solids—they have no regular structure. In amorphous solids, strong bonds between the particles hold them in position. Like crystalline solids, the particles in amorphous solids vibrate constantly. Plastic and wax are common examples of amorphous solids.

Changing States

A material can change from one state to another by being heated or cooled. Solids melt into liquids, and liquids evaporate into gases. In the opposite direction, gases condense into liquids, which then freeze into solids.

When a solid is heated, the particles begin to vibrate more strongly and move farther out of position. At a certain temperature, the particles inside the solid begin to break away

In some places, such as Yellowstone National Park, water comes out of the ground boiling hot. Like other liquids, water boils at a certain temperature. In the case of water, that temperature is 212°F (100°C). The water molecules are vibrating so strongly that some are turning into vapor and escaping from the surface as steam.

STATES OF MATTER

▼ Solid: The particles are held strongly together. The example below is a rigid crystal structure. The particles can move but only vibrate back and forth inside the crystal.

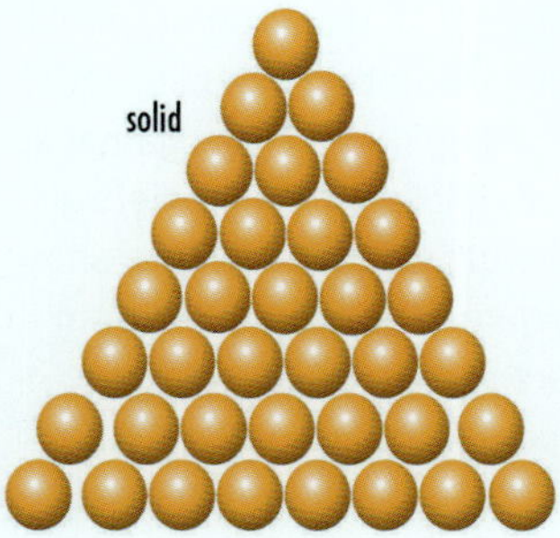

▲ Liquid: The particles are less tightly packed than in a solid. They can move past each other, so a liquid can flow into different shapes.

▼ Gas: The particles are not joined together. All move independently of each other. A gas will spread out to fill all availble space.

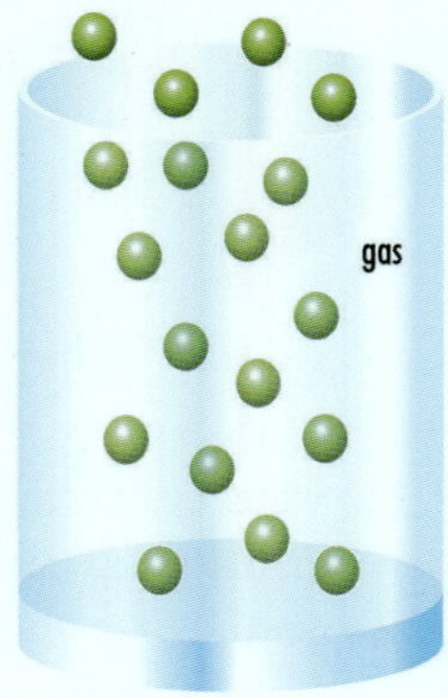

from each other. The solid's shape breaks down, and the particles can now move around more freely. The substance has become a liquid. The temperature at which a substance turns from solid to liquid is called its melting point.

The particles in a liquid are still connected to some of the others. If a liquid is heated further, the particles begin to vibrate even more quickly. Eventually they are vibrating so much that all the bonds between the particles break, and a liquid turns into a gas. The temperature at which this change occurs is called the boiling point.

As a gas, the particles are free to move in any direction. They keep moving in a straight line until they hit other gas particles, or bounce off the solid surface of a container. With the particles bouncing in all directions, the gas soon spreads out to fill the container.

KEY TERMS

Gas: State in which particles are separate and free to move in any direction.

Liquid: State in which particles are loosely bonded and are able to move freely around each other.

Solid: State in which particles are held in a rigid arrangement.

State: The form that matter takes—either a solid, a liquid, or a gas.

THREE STATES OF WATER

The water cycle comprises H_2O in all three states of matter—solid (ice), liquid (water), and gas (water vapor).

Water (H_2O) is one of the very few substances that is found naturally in all three states on Earth. Most of Earth's surface is covered in liquid H_2O, forming the oceans (**1**). The sun's heat evaporates seawater into gaseous H_2O (water vapor) that mixes with the air (**2**). When the air gets cold, the water vapor condenses into droplets of liquid or solid H_2O (ice). These gather as clouds (**3**). When the droplets get too large, they fall as rain or snow (**4**). Water also evaporates from rivers, lakes, and land to form clouds (**5**). It also seeps into the ground (**6**), or runs into the sea.

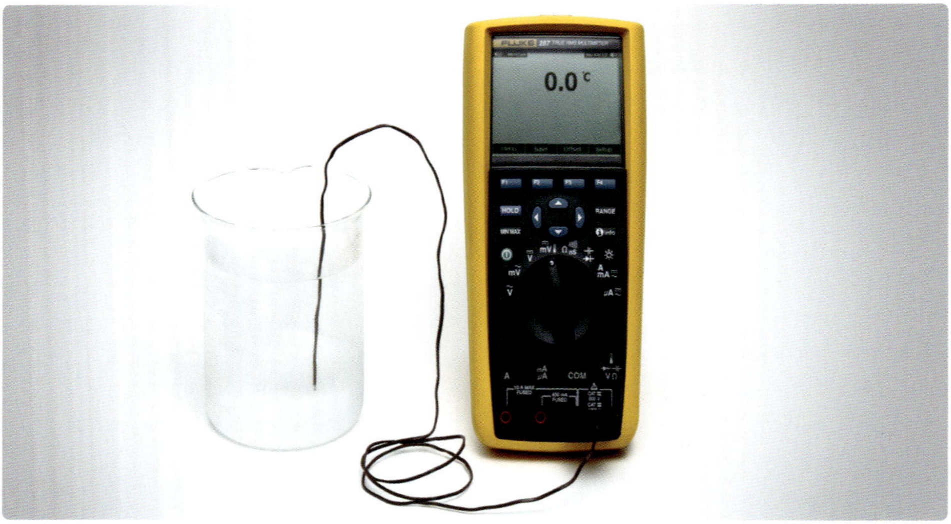

A melting solid stays at a constant temperature until all the solid has melted. Here, the ice and water remain at 32°F (0°C) until all the ice has melted.

These evaporator columns are used in the distillation process of an ethanol plant. Distillation is a technique used to separate a mixture of liquids by the differences in their boiling points. As each liquid in the mixture reaches its boiling point, it evaporates into a gas and is collected at the top of the reactor. It is then cooled back into a pure liquid.

Physical Properties of Matter

When a substance is cooled, the processes work in the opposite direction. As gas particles cool down, they move more slowly. When the particles hit each other, they are moving slowly enough to stay stuck to each other. Shapeless droplets of liquid are formed. As the liquid is cooled, its particles vibrate less strongly. They begin to connect together into the ordered structure of the solid crystal.

Melting and boiling points are physical properties of each substance. Physical properties also include color and hardness, as well as melting and boiling points. Some solids are hard, such as stone and iron, while some are soft, such as soap. However, many metals are also easy to bend, especially when hot, but stone will crack. A thin sheet of copper or aluminum, for example, can be bent easily, but a slab of stone will shatter if you try to bend it.

Salt crystals are a compound of two elements, sodium and chlorine, which have undergone a chemical reaction to form a new substance, sodium chloride.

These physical changes do not have any effect on the structure of the particles inside the substance. Whether they are joined in a crystal or floating independently as a gas, the particles stay the same. However, substances have chemical properties, too. These properties affect the way particles reorganize themselves to make completely new substances.

Chemical Changes

In the right conditions, two or more different substances will react with each other to make completely new materials. During the reaction, the atoms inside the two original substances are rearranged to form new substances. A chemical change has occurred because the original substances no longer exist. Instead, they have transformed into one or more new materials. The new substances formed by the chemical reaction have a different shape and size than the original ones. They also contain different combinations of atoms. This new combination of atoms may have very different properties than those of the starting materials. For example, solid and liquid materials might react to form a gas.

Compounds and Mixtures

When atoms of two or more elements react to form a molecule, the new substance that is formed is called a compound. The compound contains atoms of several elements. When they are combined by a chemical reaction, the compound formed generally has very different properties, both physical and chemical, from those elements.

For example, calcium carbonate ($CaCO_3$) is a compound that consists of calcium, carbon, and oxygen. Calcium is a soft metal, carbon is a nonmetal, and oxygen is a gas under ordinary conditions. Yet, when combined by a chemical reaction, they produce a crystalline substance that is used by some animals to form a hard shell. Calcium carbonate occurs in nature in the rocks known as limestone, chalk, and marble.

Compounds are different than mixtures. The calcium, carbon, and oxygen atoms are not randomly mixed together to make

↑ The shell of this snail is made of calcium carbonate. Calcium compounds are key ingredients for many animals in making bones, teeth, and shells.

ELEMENT, MIXTURE, COMPOUND

Substances exist in different forms in nature. At the most basic level are substances known as elements. Elements consist of one type of atom. These atoms may be single atoms or molecules containing a number of atoms. Mixtures occur when molecules of different substances mingle together but do not combine physically or chemically. The ingredients of a mixture can be separated from each other. Compounds are the result of a chemical reaction between two or more substances and can only be separated into individual elements by chemical methods.

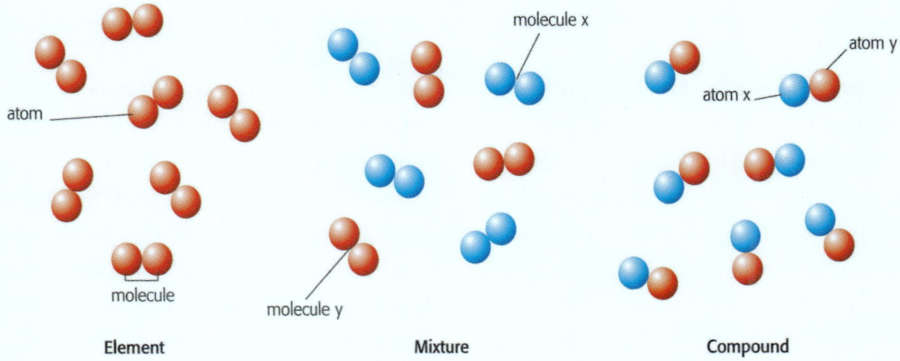

MIXING MIXTURES

Mix a small amount of sand with a similar amount of sugar. No matter how thoroughly you mix the two, you can always see the different grains of sugar and sand. This is an example of a heterogeneous mixture. Now tip the mixture into a large glass of warm water and give it a stir. Let the grains settle. What can you see? The sand sinks to the bottom, but the sugar grains have disappeared. They have dissolved into the water and have formed a solution —a homogeneous mixture.

Above left, grains of sand and sugar are mixed together next to a beaker of water. Each grain of sand and sugar is still identifiable. However, when the sand and sugar mixture has been added to water, above right, the sand sinks and the sugar dissolves completely.

calcium carbonate crystals. Each calcium carbonate formula unit is created by a chemical reaction that joins one calcium, one carbon, and three oxygen atoms together. When joined, the atoms form a completely different substance.

Different Mixtures

Inside a mixture of materials, each substance still behaves as if it were in a pure state. For example, pebbles and water can be mixed together. However, they can also easily be separated from each other. When the mixture is heated, for example, the water boils away, leaving the solid stones behind. Or the stones can simply be lifted out of the water. Mixing the two things has not changed the physical properties of either substance. However, when a compound is formed, the substances are combined by a chemical reaction.

This breakfast cereal is an example of a heterogeneous mixture. It is easy to see all the ingredients because none of them changes when put together in a bowl.

The compound has a new set of properties and it cannot easily be separated into the original starting substances.

There are two main types of mixtures: heterogeneous and homogeneous. Heterogeneous mixtures contain two or more different materials. These materials are spread unevenly throughout the mixture. A bowl of breakfast cereal is a heterogeneous mixture because it is easy to see the different materials—the cereal and milk—that the bowl contains.

It is harder to determine what is included in a homogeneous mixture. That is because all the ingredients are evenly mixed up so that you cannot identify one from the other. For example, butter is a homogeneous mixture of water and fat. Many homogeneous mixtures involve water. Another example is a cup of coffee. The molecules in the coffee granules, which give the drink its taste and color, are evenly mixed up with the water molecules. When a spoonful of sugar is added, the sugar molecules also become part of the homogeneous mixture. It is impossible to tell the different ingredients apart.

Chemists describe a mixture like this as a solution. The water is called the solvent, and the coffee and sugar are called the solutes because they dissolve in the solvent.

KEY TERMS

Compound: Matter made from more than one element which has undergone a chemical reaction.

Heterogeneous mixture: A mixture in which different substances are spread unevenly throughout.

Homogeneous mixture: A mixture in which one substance has dissolved or been completely mixed into another.

Mixture: Matter made from different types of substances that are not physically or chemically bonded together.

CHAPTER 2

The Elements

All matter consists of elements. Chemical elements are each formed from one sort of substance. They cannot be easily broken down into smaller parts. Scientists organize the elements in rows and columns called the Periodic Table.

Not all atoms are the same. There are about 90 types of atoms that occur naturally on Earth, and they make up the most basic substances called elements. Three-quarters of the elements are metals. Ten other elements are gases in normal conditions, while just two (including one of the metals) are liquids. Some elements will react with just about all the others, while a few rarely react at all. It is possible that more than those 90 elements occur elsewhere in the universe, but these only last for a short time before breaking down into more stable elements. None of these unstable elements exist naturally on Earth anymore. Scientists have made some of them in laboratories, but they can only produce very tiny amounts at a time, and the elements quickly break down.

Bismuth is a rare metallic element with a regular crystalline structure. It has a silvery-pink color. On its own, bismuth is brittle. It is usually mixed with other metals to make it useful.

ELEMENTS ON EARTH

The most common element in the universe is hydrogen. Hydrogen atoms are the smallest and simplest of all atoms. Three-quarters of all matter in the universe is made of hydrogen.

The most common element on Earth is iron. Much of the planet's core is made of this metal. However, the most common elements on the surface of Earth are silicon and oxygen. For example, silicon dioxide is the main compound in sand and is also found in most rocks. Other elements are very rare. Scientists estimate that there are just a few grams of astatine in all of Earth's rocks put together.

Earth is made of several layers comprising different elements and compounds. Iron is the most common element on Earth and may be either solid or liquid, depending on pressure and temperature.

Understanding Elements

People have long understood that certain basic substances can be combined to make new and completely different substances. Today, chemists understand how atoms are constructed and what makes each element different from the next. However, before science provided these explanations, people had very different ideas about elements.

For many hundreds of years, people thought that everything in the world was made from just four "elements": earth, fire, water, and air. The way these elements were supposed to work had more to do with magic than science. Nevertheless, the idea of elements as fundamental substances was not incorrect; it was just that nobody had discovered any of the true elements.

The Birth of Chemistry

The first people to investigate how materials could be changed into other substances were not chemists but alchemists. Alchemists are first recorded working in Egypt and China

ALCHEMY AND SCIENCE

Alchemists were very different from modern chemists. Chemists are scientists and they share their discoveries with others. Chemists check each other's discoveries to make sure they are correct and then use them to learn more about how atoms and molecules behave. In contrast, the main goal of an alchemist was to find one of three things: the elixir, a drink that could make a person live forever; the panacea, a medicine that could cure all illnesses; and the philosopher's stone, which could turn any metal into gold. Obviously these discoveries would have made an alchemist hugely powerful. As a result, alchemists preferred to keep their work private. They recorded things in code, using secret symbols.

One of the most influential alchemists was an Arab man named Jābir ibn Hayyan, also known as Geber. His writings are very confusing and often contradict each other.

This painting depicts an alchemist surrounded by the apparatus, instruments, and books of magic that he would use to carry out experiments and create potions in his workshop. In the 18th century, as scientific knowledge increased, alchemy began to be replaced by chemistry.

about 2,500 years ago. Alchemists were not scientists, and much of what they did is often remembered as the work of wizards and witches. They made potions and remedies and thought that matter could be transformed using magic.

This book on magic was published in 1658. In the corners are representations of the "four elements": fire, air, earth, and water. Clockwise from top left, fire is represented by a salamander; air by birds and wind; water by sea creatures; and earth by animals.

KEY TERMS

Alchemist: Person who attempted to change one substance into another using a combination of primitive chemistry and magic.
Four elements: The ancient theory that all matter consisted of only four elements (earth, air, fire, and water) and their combinations.

↑ Mercury is a metallic element. It is one of only two elements that are liquid at room temperature—the other is bromine.

Unlike chemists, alchemists did not carry out proper scientific experiments. They also did not understand many of the basic ideas of chemistry, such as the difference between a compound and a mixture. However, they did make some important discoveries. Alchemists began to understand that there were many more than just four elements. They identified several metal elements, such as mercury, iron, and gold.

Alchemists also correctly thought that sulfur, arsenic, and other nonmetals were elements. They began to use symbols for each of the elements, and modern chemists do the same. However, nobody really understood that elements were made of atoms and formed compounds until chemists began to investigate elemental properties in a scientific way.

Ancient Greeks

Atoms have only been detected by scientists in the last 200 years or so. However, people have been talking about atoms for thousands of years. The first people to think atoms existed were ancient Greek philosophers. Unlike alchemists, philosophers did not perform experiments to try and understand matter. They did not use science to prove their ideas, either. Instead, they came up with theories that seemed to match the way they observed nature working.

The word "atom" comes from the Greek word *atomos*, which means "indivisible." The first person to suggest that matter is made of atoms was Leucippus of Miletus, who lived about 2,500 years ago. He thought atoms were all the same and could not be squeezed, stretched, or broken. Leucippus thought atoms had to exist because things were constantly changing in nature. However, he understood that something new could not be made from nothing, so he suggested that all changes were just atoms being rearranged. The atoms themselves

SEEING ATOMS

There is a way of making a picture of the atoms on the surface of a substance. This requires a machine called a scanning tunneling microscope. The microscope has a metal probe with an ultrafine point. At the tip of this point is a single atom. The probe works by picking up an electric current from the atoms it is detecting. It can be used only to investigate substances that conduct electricity, such as metals.

The probe is lowered to just above the surface of an object. When the tip of the probe moves close to an atom, the current running through it rises. The atoms of certain elements produce larger bursts of electricity than others. A computer uses the rises and falls in the current to create a picture of where all the atoms are on the surface.

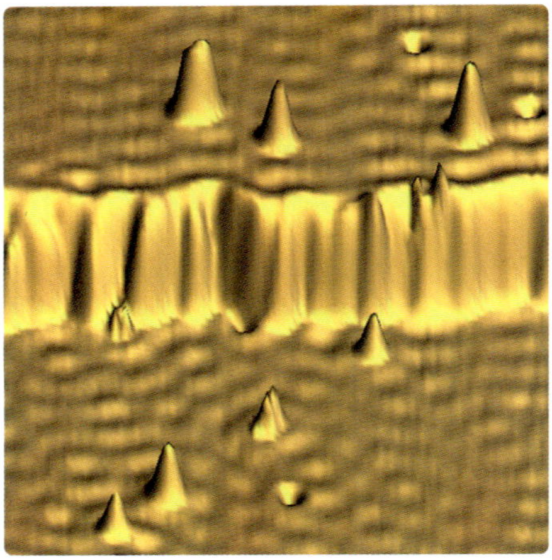

← A scanning tunneling microscope image shows interactions between cobalt and silver atoms and a copper surface.

could not be changed, only the way they were organized. Leucippus and his followers did not understand anything about how atoms are constructed or why they behave the way they do. However, their atom theory was correct in many ways.

Scientific Approach

When chemists began to study substances in a scientific way, they began to realize that matter was indeed made of atoms, but that not all atoms were the same. John Dalton (1766–1844) was an English scientist who made one of the greatest discoveries in chemistry. At the beginning of the 19th century, he noticed that when two types of gases were mixed together, they did not behave as a single cloud that filled its container. Leucippus had said that all things were made up of identical atoms, so the question was, why were the atoms in each gas behaving differently?

Dalton saw that both gases expanded independently of each other, so they were both spread evenly throughout the container. This simple observation proved that not all atoms were the same, as Leucippus had believed. The two gases therefore must contain different types of atoms that behaved in a different way from each other.

The Guggenheim Museum in Bilbao, Spain, is covered with a thin layer of the metallic element titanium. Titanium is one of the 25 elements that had been discovered by the early 19th century.

Mass and Density

By the early 19th century, scientists had identified about 25 elements. These included metals such as gold, mercury, and copper, which had been known for centuries. There were also new additions, including oxygen, which had been discovered a few years before Dalton's experiment. Dalton suggested that each element had its own type of atom.

The main difference Dalton could find between the various elements was their mass (how much matter the substance contains) and density (how much mass something has at a particular volume). He figured out how heavy an element was by reacting it with a fixed mass of another element. He then weighed what was produced and could calculate how heavy the first element was compared with the second. The extra mass of the new compound indicated how heavy the added atoms were. With this measurement, Dalton could begin to figure out how heavy each type of atom was in relation to all the others.

Dalton also showed that compounds formed from even proportions of elements. For example, a compound could contain equal amounts of two elements, or have twice as much of one than the other. However, the proportions of each ingredient were always whole numbers. You never find one atom of an element joined to one and a half atoms of another element.

English scientist John Dalton was the first person to propose that atoms of different elements do not all behave the same way.

KEY TERMS

Chemical symbol: The letters that represent a chemical, such as "Cl" for chlorine or "Na" for sodium.

Chemical formula: The letters and numbers that represent a chemical compound, such as "H_2O" for water.

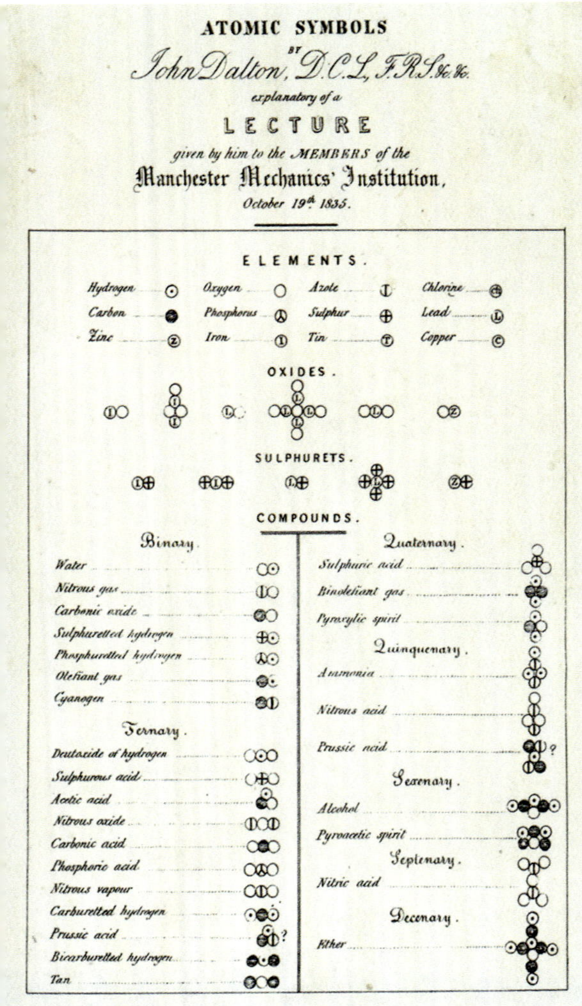

Symbols And Formulas

Although he did not know it at the time, Dalton was describing how atoms are arranged inside a compound. A simple compound such as sodium chloride is produced when equal amounts of sodium and chlorine atoms react together. The proportions of each element, or ratio, is 1:1. However, other compounds have more complicated ratios of elements. For example, water is formed when hydrogen and oxygen react. Twice as many hydrogen atoms are needed than oxygen atoms. So the compound has a ratio of 2:1.

Chemists use these proportions to explain the exact ingredients of molecules. Like alchemists before them, chemists use symbols for each element. However, they have chosen ones that are much easier to understand. The symbol of hydrogen is H; chlorine is Cl; and oxygen has the symbol O. Some elements have less obvious symbols because they are taken from languages other than English. For example, sodium has the symbol Na, which comes from the Latin word "natrium." Iron has the symbol Fe from "ferrum," the Latin word for iron.

← This table of elements, compounds, and chemical symbols was created by English scientist John Dalton and printed for one of his lectures in 1835. Each circular symbol represents one atom, and molecules are represented by combinations of these symbols. This system is no longer used, but many of Dalton's ideas were essentially correct.

Chemists combine the symbols and the proportions to make chemical formulas. These are a way of describing what proportions of elements a compound contains. For example, the formula for sodium chloride is NaCl. Water has the formula H_2O. The subscript 2 indicates that in each molecule of water, two hydrogen atoms are joined with one oxygen atom. More complicated compounds, such as glucose (which is a type of sugar), have large molecules that contain many atoms. The formula for glucose is $C_6H_{12}O_6$.

FORMULAS

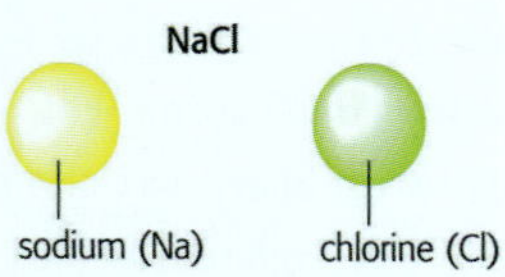

A sodium atom (Na) combines with a chlorine atom (Cl) to form the basic structural unit of the sodium chloride crystal structure (NaCl). This compound is common salt.

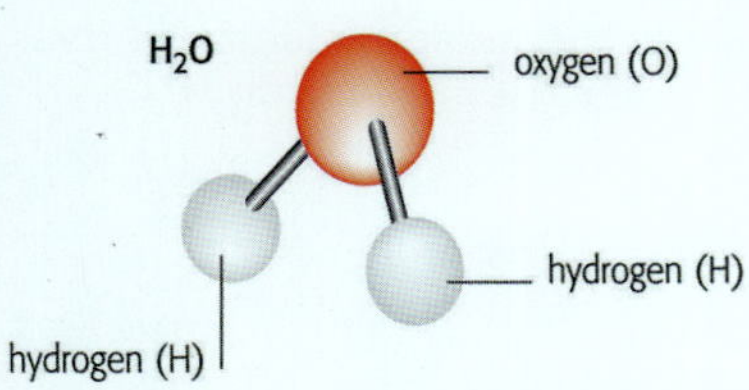

A single oxygen atom (O) combines with two hydrogen atoms (2H) to produce a water molecule (H_2O).

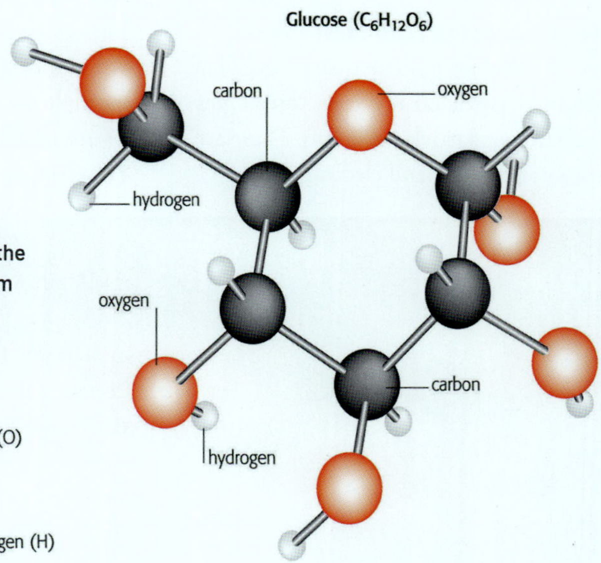

Glucose is a type of sugar. This complex molecule is made of six carbon atoms (6C), twelve hydrogen atoms (12H), and six oxygen atoms (6O). Together, these form $C_6H_{12}O_6$.

CHAPTER 3

Atomic Structure

The atoms of different elements differ from each other, but they have a common structure. Discovering this structure was one of the greatest scientific breakthroughs.

For hundreds of years, scientists thought that atoms were the smallest particles of matter. In the 20th century, scientists began to realize that atoms were made of even smaller particles called subatomic particles. There are three types of subatomic particles in atoms. These are protons, neutrons, and electrons.

All atoms are constructed using these particles, which are always arranged following the same rules. An element's physical and chemical properties are set by the number of particles in its atoms. For example, an element with many particles in its atoms will have a very high density. However, an element with just a few

Elements are formed by the stars. As stars burn, they create new elements. When a star explodes as a supernova, these new elements are flung out into space. The red ring of this supernova shows the presence of oxygen and neon.

MINUTE PARTICLES

Subatomic particles are very small. One gram of electrons contains more than 1,000 times more individual particles than there are stars in the universe. (There are more than 200 billion trillion stars total.) Scientists now know that tiny subatomic particles are made of even smaller ones called quarks. The largest atoms are about five millionths of a millimeter across, but the nucleus is a few trillionths of a millimeter across. That's like a ping-pong ball in the center of a football field.

particles in its atoms will have a low density. Similarly, the number of particles in an element's atoms governs how reactive the element is.

NUCLEUS

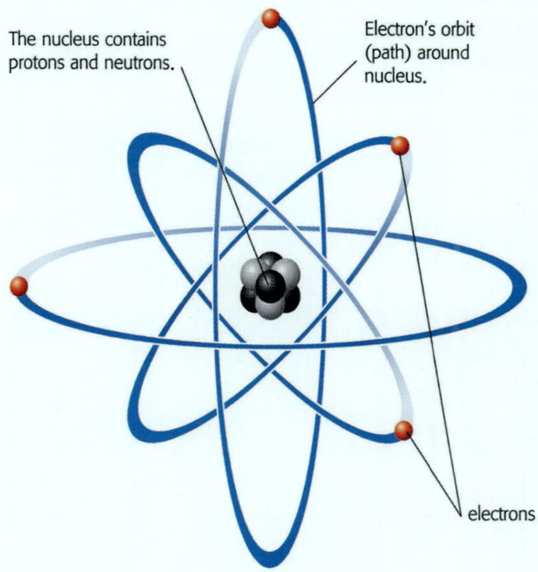

An atom is mostly empty space. The protons and neutrons are gathered in the central region called the nucleus. Electrons move around outside the nucleus.

Looking at Protons

The inside of an atom is mostly empty space, and the particles inside it are incredibly small. At the center is a tiny core called the nucleus (plural: nuclei). The nucleus contains the first type of particle: the proton. The name proton was first used to describe this particle around 1920 and comes from the Greek word for "first." The proton was given this name because it was the first particle to be found inside an atom. (Electrons were discovered in 1897, but they were not known to be part of atoms until after the discovery of protons.)

The number of protons in an atom defines the type of element. The simplest and smallest type of atoms—those of hydrogen—have just a single proton in their nucleus. Larger atoms have more protons in the nucleus. For example, the largest

COMMON ELEMENTS

This table shows the subatomic particles of the most common isotopes (see page 32) of the first 14 elements in the periodic table. The number of neutrons is not always the same as the number of protons. The atomic mass number is the sum of the atomic number and the number of neutrons.

	Number of protons (atomic number)	Number of neutrons	Number of electrons	Atomic mass number
Hydrogen	1	0	1	1
Helium	2	2	2	4
Lithium	3	4	3	7
Beryllium	4	5	4	9
Boron	5	6	5	11
Carbon	6	6	6	12
Nitrogen	7	7	7	14
Oxygen	8	8	8	16
Fluorine	9	9	9	18
Neon	10	10	10	20
Sodium	11	12	11	23
Magnesium	12	12	12	24
Aluminum	13	14	13	27
Silicon	14	14	14	28

naturally occurring element is the metal uranium. Uranium atoms have 92 protons. The number of protons in an atom is called the atomic number. Each element has a unique number of protons in its nucleus. If two atoms have different atomic numbers, then they belong to different elements.

Protons have a positive electrical charge. This charge is a fundamental property of protons, and each one has an identical charge. Chemists describe the charge of each proton as +1.

← Aluminum has many common uses, such as in soft drink cans. Each of the tiny aluminum atoms has a nucleus of 13 protons and 14 neutrons surrounded by 13 electrons.

KEY TERMS

Atomic mass number: The number of protons and neutrons that are in an atom's nucleus.
Atomic number: The number of protons that are in a nucleus.
Electron: A small, negatively charged subatomic particle that moves around the nucleus.
Neutron: A subatomic particle with no charge located in an atom's nucleus.
Nucleus: The central part of an atom, made of protons and neutrons.
Proton: A positively charged particle found in an atom's nucleus.
Subatomic particles: Particles that are smaller than an atom.

A proton's charge is linked to the way it pushes and pulls on other particles inside the atom. Because of the protons in it, a nucleus always has a positive charge. The nucleus of a larger atom contains a lot of protons. The charges of these particles add up to make a positive charge that is stronger than that of a smaller nucleus with fewer protons.

Take a Look at Neutrons

With the exception of hydrogen, all elements have a second type of particle in their nuclei. These are called neutrons. Neutrons are slightly heavier than protons. However, they have no electrical charge—they are neutral. The simplest element to have neutrons in its atoms is helium. This has two protons in the nucleus and two neutrons. The number of neutrons in larger atoms is also roughly the same as the number of protons. However, this varies from element to element. The number of particles in an atom's nucleus—protons plus neutrons—is called the atomic mass number.

PROTONS, NEUTRONS, ELECTRONS

The number of protons in the nucleus of an atom determines the type of element the atom is. The number of neutrons is usually similar to the number of protons but is not always the same. Protons and electrons have an electric charge. The protons are positively charged and the electrons are negatively charged. Neutrons are electrically neutral; they have no charge.

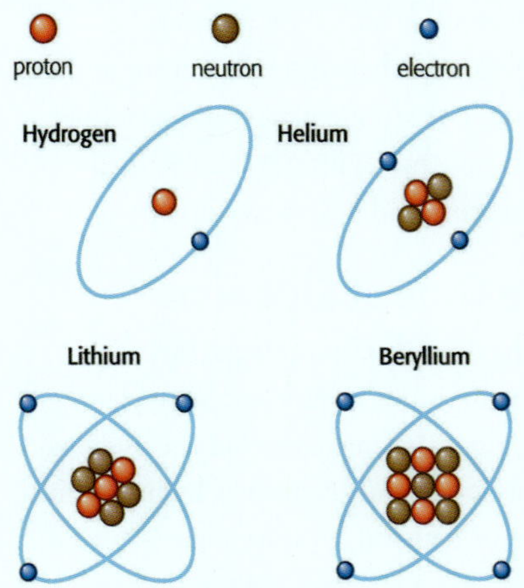

The reddish color in the rocks of the Grand Canyon is caused by iron in the rocks. Iron is a common constituent of many rocks. Iron atoms do not all have the same atomic mass number. Around 90 percent of iron atoms have a mass number of 56. The remaining 10 percent have different atomic mass numbers because they have different numbers of neutrons in their nucleus.

For example, most hydrogen atoms have an atomic mass number of 1 (1 proton plus 0 neutrons) and most carbon atoms have atomic mass numbers of 12 (6 protons and 6 neutrons). The atomic mass number tells scientists how much matter is contained inside an atom and how heavy it is.

Take a Look at Electrons

The third type of subatomic particle, the electron, is not located in the nucleus. Instead, electrons move around the nucleus. Electrons are about 1,830 times lighter than a proton or neutron. Despite their small size, electrons have a negative electrical charge of –1. This charge is exactly equal and opposite to the charge of each proton. Particles with opposite charges attract each other, and the negatively charged electrons are pulled toward the positively charged nucleus. This force keeps the electrons in position and holds the atom together. The number of electrons in an atom is always the same as the number of protons. For example, hydrogen atoms have one electron, while helium atoms have two. Therefore, the positive charge of the protons is balanced exactly by the charge of the electrons. As a result, whole atoms never have an overall charge.

DISCOVERING ATOMIC STRUCTURE

Electrons were discovered in 1897, and protons were first isolated in 1910, though they were not given the name proton until around 10 years later. Neutrons were discovered in 1932. At first, scientists thought that atoms were more or less solid arrangements of protons, with the smaller electrons positioned in between to balance out the particles' different charges.

However, in 1911, Ernest Rutherford (1871–1937), a New Zealander working in England, showed that protons were actually located in a tiny nucleus at the center of the atom. He discovered this by firing a beam of alpha particles at a very thin sheet of gold. (An alpha particle is the nucleus of a helium atom that has lost its electrons. It has two protons and two neutrons and is positively charged.) Most of the alpha particles went straight through the gold, but some were deflected and others bounced back. Rutherford realized that the particles that were changing direction were being repelled by other positively charged particles inside the atom.
He discovered that the beam of particles was only affected by tiny areas of the gold sheet, areas smaller than the individual atoms. He realized this meant protons, the positively charged parts of atoms, only occupied a tiny area at the center of the atom, which he called the nucleus.

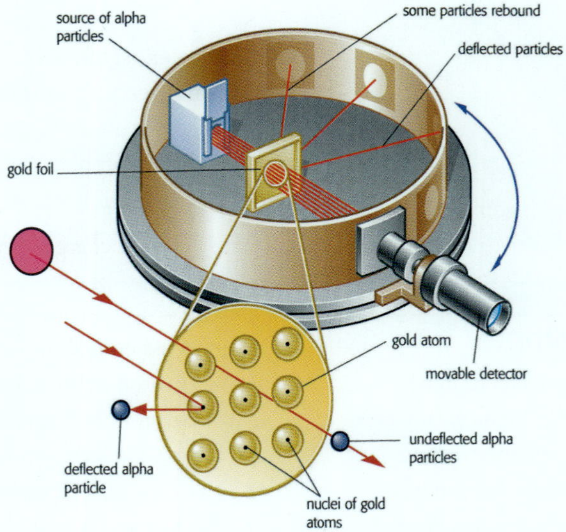

In Rutherford's experiment, a beam of alpha particles (helium nuclei) is fired at a thin film of gold foil. This is contained within a vacuum so that the alpha particles do not rebound from air particles. A movable detector swivels around the gold foil and measures the quantity of alpha particles that pass through the foil or are deflected by the foil. Most pass straight through, some are deflected, and a small number rebound.

CARBON DATING

Some isotopes are radioactive—they decay into other isotopes or elements over time. Radioactive isotopes can be used to tell how old an ancient object is. Different isotopes are used for different ages. For example, potassium-40 (K-40) is used to date rocks that are billions of years old. Carbon-14 (C-14) is used to calculate the age of once-living things, such as wood, bones, and even clothing made from natural material. Carbon is an essential ingredient of all living things. Scientists know that when living material is formed, it always contains a certain proportion of C-14 atoms. Over many years, these atoms break down, so the proportion of C-14 in the material falls. By measuring the amount of C-14 in the remains of a living thing, scientists can figure out almost exactly how many years ago it was alive. This technique can be used for dating objects up to 50,000 years old.

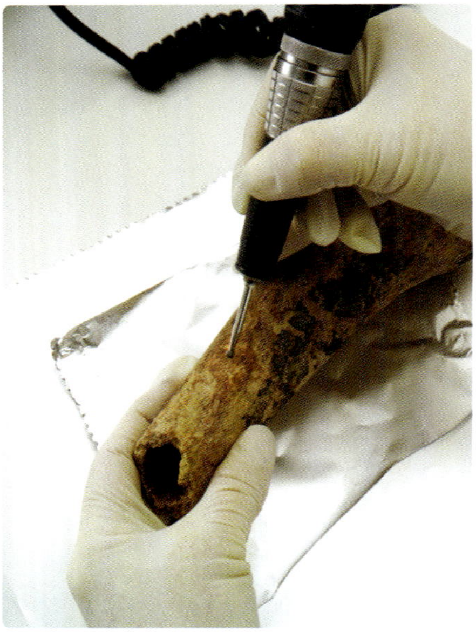

A scientist takes a sample from a bone and then measures the proportion of carbon-14 to carbon-12. From this data, the scientist can estimate the age of the sample fairly accurately. The scientist wears gloves to prevent contamination with living tissue.

Looking at Isotopes

All the atoms of one element must have the same atomic number. However, atoms of the same element can have slightly different atomic mass numbers. That is because an element can have different numbers of neutrons in its nucleus.

The different versions of an element are called isotopes. Hydrogen atoms, for example, exist as three isotopes. Most of them are simple hydrogen atoms with an atomic mass number of 1 (they have a single proton in the nucleus). About 0.015 percent of hydrogen atoms have a neutron as well as a proton in the nucleus. This isotope has an atomic mass number of 2 and is named deuterium, or heavy hydrogen.

Finally, one in every billion trillion hydrogen atoms is the isotope tritium. This has two neutrons in the nucleus, so it has an atomic mass number of 3.

ISOTOPES

Hydrogen exists as three isotopes. By far the most common isotope is ($^{1}_{1}H$). This has only a single proton in its nucleus and no neutrons. Deuterium ($^{2}_{1}H$) and tritium ($^{3}_{1}H$) are much rarer. They have one and two neutrons in their nucleus, respectively. Unlike the isotopes of hydrogen, most isotopes do not have special names and are therefore identified by their atomic number, such as carbon-12 ($^{12}_{6}C$) and carbon-14 ($^{14}_{6}C$). The number of electrons does not change in different isotopes of the same element. The electron number remains the same as that of the atomic number (proton number).

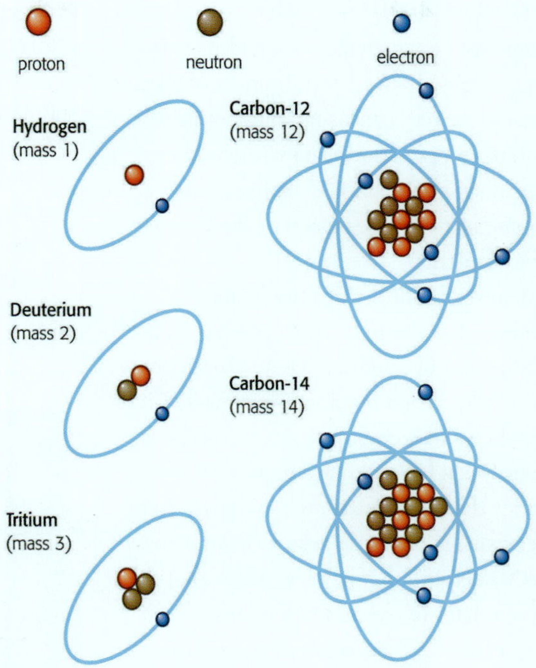

Isotopes Notation

To ensure that people know what isotope an atom is, an atom's atomic mass number is always written above its symbol, and the atomic number is displayed below it. For example the main isotope of carbon is displayed as 126 C). This isotope is also described as carbon-12 (C-12).

The atoms of both deuterium and tritium are radioactive. This means that their nuclei are unstable and they quickly break apart, releasing radiation. Many of the less common isotopes of other elements are radioactive, too.

Atomic Mass

Chemists use a system of atomic masses based on the mass of each element that will react with a known mass of another. In effect, they are using an average mass based on the relative amount of each isotope of an element present. For example, most hydrogen atoms have an atomic mass number of 1, but a tiny amount of the element's atoms have atomic mass numbers of 2 and 3. Therefore the average atomic mass number for all hydrogen atoms is very slightly higher than 1 (1.00794, to be precise). This number is the element's atomic mass.

To keep things simple, chemists often round down hydrogen's atomic mass to just 1.

Average Atomic Mass

Atoms are extremely light—a hydrogen atom weighs about 1.7 septillionths of a gram. It would be very confusing to use units this small to compare one atom with another. Instead, an atom's mass is expressed as a comparison with the masses of the atoms of other elements.

Chemists do this using atomic mass numbers. For example, hydrogen has an atomic mass of 1, helium has an atomic mass of 4, while carbon has an atomic mass of 12. This shows that carbon atoms are 12 times heavier than hydrogen atoms and 3 times heavier than helium atoms. Chemists often refer to atomic mass as relative atomic mass (RAM) because that name explains that the figure relates to the other elements.

Molecules contain more than one atom, and their mass is also important. This mass is measured as the total of the atomic masses of the atoms in the molecule. This adds up

KEY TERMS

Mole: The number of atoms in 12 grams of carbon-12 atoms. This number is 602,213,670,000,000,000,000,000 (6.022×10^{23}).

Relative atomic mass (RAM): A measure of the mass of an atom compared with the mass of another atom. The values used are the same as those for atomic mass.

Relative molecular mass (RMM): The sum of all the atomic masses of the atoms in a molecule.

These blue crystals are made of molecules of copper sulfate ($CuSO_4$). The relative molecular mass (RMM) for copper sulfate can be calculated by adding the relative atomic masses (RAM) of each element. Copper (Cu) has a RAM of 64, sulfur (S) 32, and oxygen (O) 16. So taking into account that $CuSO_4$ has four oxygen atoms, the RMM is $64 + 32 + (4 \times 16) = 160$.

MASS SPECTROMETER

The atoms of each element contain a certain set amount of matter. Chemists can use this fact to identify the ingredients of almost any material. They do this with a mass spectrometer. This is a machine that can detect the size of atoms and molecules inside a substance and calculate their proportions.

First the material is turned into a gas. The atoms and molecules in the gas are given a positive charge by ripping away some of their electrons using a strong electric current. The charged gas is formed into a beam by the injection magnet.

The beam is then accelerated and fired through an analyzer magnet. This magnet makes the particles in the beam change direction. Lighter particles are deflected more than heavier ones. The particles then crash into a detector.

Scientists can tell how heavy a particle is by where it hits the detector. Once they know how heavy the particle is, they can figure out what type of atoms (or combination of atoms) it contains. They can then figure out what sort of substances were present in the sample.

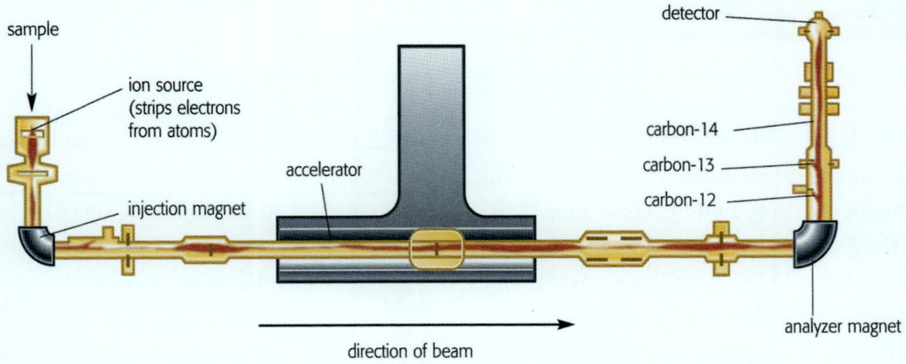

This mass spectrometer is measuring how much of a sample is made of carbon-12, carbon-13, and carbon-14. The resulting data can be used for carbon dating.

into the relative molecular mass (RMM). For example, a water molecule has two hydrogen atoms (atomic mass 1) and one oxygen atom (atomic mass 16). Therefore water's RMM is 18 (1+1+16).

Knowing the RAMs and RMMs of different substances helps chemists figure out how those substances must have combined and altered during chemical reactions.

HOW MANY MOLECULES?

Water has an RMM of 18. One mole of water has a mass of 18 grams (0.6 ounces). You can use this to calculate how many molecules a cup of water contains. Weigh an empty cup on a kitchen scale; using grams makes it easier. Pour some water into the cup and see how much heavier it is. The difference is the mass of the water. Divide this mass in grams by 18 to get the number of moles of water in the cup. Then multiply this figure by Avogadro's number (see below) to calculate the number of molecules. For example, if the water has a mass of 36 grams, then there are 2 moles that contain 1,204,000,000,000,000,000,000,000 molecules, or 1.204 septillion, in total.

If this beaker has a mass of 10 grams, then the water has a mass of 90 grams. This mass of water divided by 18 is 5. Therefore there must be 5 moles of water in the beaker.

Using Moles to Measure

Chemists measure amounts of elements and compounds using a unit called a mole. This is defined as 12 grams (0.42 ounces) of carbon-12 atoms. (The RAM of this isotope is 12). Chemists chose this isotope to define the mole because carbon is a common element on Earth. One mole of any element has a mass equivalent to its atomic mass expressed in grams. For example, one mole of hydrogen has a mass of 1 gram (0.035 ounces), while one mole of lead, which has an atomic mass of 207, has a mass of 207 grams (7.3 ounces).

A mole of anything contains the same number of particles or pieces—that is, 602,213,670,000,000,000,000,000. This number is more often written as 6.022×10^{23}, which means 6.022 multiplied by 10, 23 times. This is more than the number of stars there are thought to be in the entire universe or grains of sand on Earth. This number is called Avogadro's number. It is named for the Italian scientist Amedeo Avogadro (1776–1856). Avogadro suggested that equal quantities of gases at a fixed temperature and pressure always contain the same number of atoms or molecules. Therefore, a gallon of hydrogen gas contains the same number of atoms as a gallon of oxygen gas. However, the gallon of oxygen has a mass 16 times more than the gallon of hydrogen.

Using Avogadro's number, relative atomic mass numbers, and relative molecular mass numbers, scientists can easily figure out the number of atoms or molecules that exist in a given sample.

AMEDEO AVOGADRO

Amedeo Avogadro was born in Turin, Italy, on August 9, 1776. His father, Count Filippo Avogadro, was a lawyer, and Amedeo also trained as a lawyer. However, he became increasingly interested in physics and mathematics. In 1806, he was appointed demonstrator at the Academy of Turin. In 1811, he published a paper in which he suggested that equal volumes of gases at the same temperature and pressure contain the same number of molecules. This paper later had a great influence on chemistry, although it was many years before the importance of his work was widely recognized. Avogadro's number is named in honor of his important contribution to the understanding of atoms and molecules, though he had no knowledge of this number or of the mole.

These samples of compounds all contain 1 mole of each substance.

CHAPTER 4

Understanding Electrons

Electrons play a vital role in chemical reactions. They are found outside the atom's nucleus. Their positions influence how easily an atom will combine and react with other atoms.

While most of an atom's matter is locked up in the dense nucleus at the center, most of its behavior is controlled by the tiny electrons that move around the nucleus. For example, electrons are the parts of the atom that are involved in chemical reactions.

Arranging Electrons

Each electron in an atom has its own position. The electrons repel each other and never come into contact. They are also arranged in layers called electron shells. Different atoms have a different number of shells, depending on how many electrons the

The sun releases particles that travel through space as solar wind. When a solar wind stream hits Earth, the particles in the solar wind collide with gas atoms in the atmosphere. The collisions knock the electrons in the atoms into another shell, emitting energy in the form of colored light as they go. These lights can be seen in the skies near the North and South Poles and are called auroras.

ELECTRON SHELLS

There is a strict order in which electrons fill the shells that surround the nucleus of an atom. Hydrogen, the first element in the periodic table, has only one electron orbiting its nucleus. Helium, the second element, has two. Because the inner shell is very close to the nucleus, it can only hold two electrons. The next element is lithium, which has three electrons. Since the inner shell is full, the third electron has to orbit in the next shell. The second shell can hold a maximum of eight electrons. Atoms with full outer shells are stable and unreactive. Lithium needs seven electrons and carbon needs four electrons to be stable.

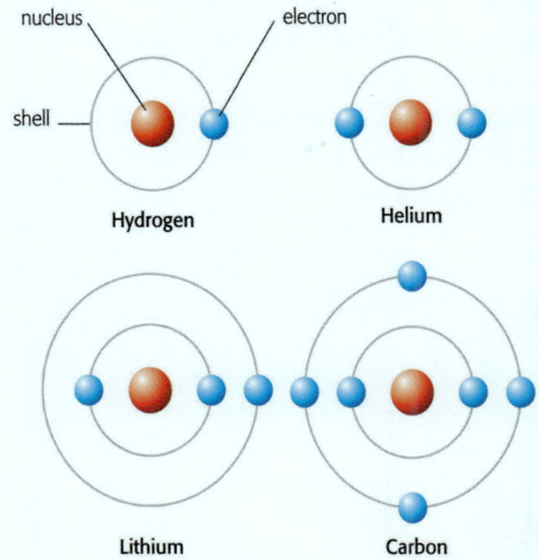

atom has. For example, hydrogen has just a single shell, containing its only electron. However, the atoms of uranium, the largest element, have their 92 electrons arranged in seven shells. The shell nearest the nucleus is the smallest. Shells get larger and can hold more electrons as they get farther away from the center of the atom.

Shell Layers

Electron shells are also sometimes described as energy levels. The electrons in the shell nearest to the nucleus have the lowest amount of energy, and those farthest away have the highest. When an atom receives some energy, such as when it is heated, its electrons move to a higher energy level farther away from the nucleus.

↑ Niels Bohr was the Danish scientist who first suggested that electrons orbit the nuclei of atoms in shells. That idea was key to understanding atomic structure.

KEY TERMS

Shell: The orbit of an electron. Each shell can contain a specific number of electrons and no more.
Energy level: The shells each represent a different energy level. Those closest to the nucleus have the lowest energy.

The rays of visible light are caused by tiny particles called photons. Photons are created when the electrons that surround atoms change their energy level.

Atoms release energy when their electrons drop down to lower energy levels and move back toward the nucleus. This model of how an atom works was suggested by Niels Bohr (1885–1962), a Danish physicist, in 1913. It is still seen as one of the best ways to understand atoms.

Types of Radiation

Bohr's description of electron shells explains how light and other types of radiation are produced by atoms. Light is just one type of electromagnetic radiation. Others include radio waves, heat, ultraviolet light, and X-rays. All these types of radiation are produced in the same way, but some involve greater quantities of energy than others. Visible light lies in the middle of the spectrum—the name given to the range of radiation types. Some rays of light contain more energy than others. Our eyes see these differences as color. Blue light has more energy than yellow light, which has more than red light. Ultraviolet (UV) light and X-rays are two examples of radiation that have more energy than visible light. UV is the invisible radiation in sunlight that causes sunburn and tanning. X-rays are used to take images of bones inside the body. Heat, also known as infrared radiation, contains less energy than light, as do radio waves.

Photon Particles

Most electromagnetic radiation is released from atoms. When an electron drops down an energy level, the atom releases a tiny particle called a photon. This particle is even smaller and lighter than an electron. Rays of light or other radiation are streams of photons being produced by atoms.

The photon carries the radiation's energy. The amount of energy it carries depends on how many energy levels the electron has dropped. If the electron has moved from a high energy level a long way from the nucleus into a shell nearer the nucleus, then the photon will carry high-energy radiation such as X-rays. Smaller drops release less energy.

PHOTONS

When an atom receives energy in the form of heat or light, electrons in its inner shells (**a**) are boosted to a shell that has higher energy levels (**b**).

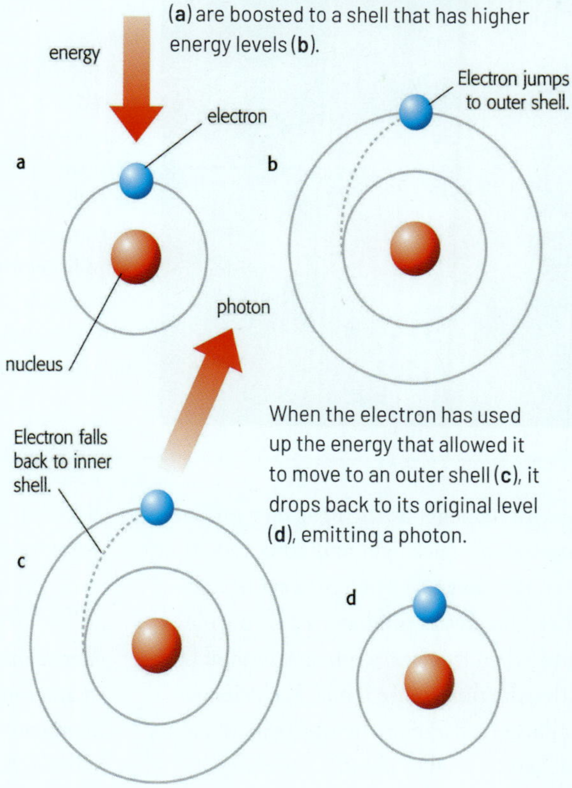

When the electron has used up the energy that allowed it to move to an outer shell (**c**), it drops back to its original level (**d**), emitting a photon.

Energy Levels

The energy levels in an atom are fixed. They depend on the atom's size. Electrons can only move between energy levels. They cannot move halfway between two levels. As a result, when they drop down levels, they always release photons with exactly the same amount of energy. This amount of energy is called a quantum. Quanta (the plural of quantum) are fixed amounts of energy. It is not possible for an atom to release half a quantum. This fact forms the basis of quantum physics, the branch of science that investigates the forces that govern atoms.

Because atoms can only release a certain set of fixed amounts of energy, chemists can

KEY TERMS

Electromagnetic radiation: The energy emitted by a source such as X-rays, ultraviolet light, visible light, heat, or radio waves.
Photon: A particle that carries a quantity of energy, usually in the form of light.

FIREWORKS

Fireworks contain small amounts of explosives that blow up to produce a display of colors. The colors in fireworks are produced by certain chemicals that are mixed into the explosives. When the firework explodes, the atoms in these chemicals react with each other or the air and release energy as colored light. The color of the light depends on the elements in the firework.

If a firework contains potassium compounds, it will explode with a purple color. Lithium produces a red color. Blue sparkles are caused by metals such as copper and cobalt.

identify elements by the light they produce. Elements produce light and other radiation when they burn or when they are heated. Potassium always produces a pale purple flame when it burns, while magnesium burns with a dazzling white flame. Each element produces a characteristic spectrum of colors that can be used to identify the element.

Chemical Reactions

Electrons are the parts of an atom that take part in chemical reactions. When atoms connect, they lose, gain, or share their electrons with other atoms. The interaction of electrons creates the forces that hold the atoms together as molecules. Some elements are more likely to react and form compounds than others. Whether an element is reactive depends on how its electrons are arranged around the nucleus. The arrangement of electrons controls how easy it is for an atom to lose, gain, or share its electrons.

Distribution of Electrons

The electrons in the outermost shell of an atom are the ones that take part in chemical reactions. Electron shells are most stable when they are completely full. The atoms of most elements have an outer shell that is only partially full. Lithium atoms have just one electron in their second shell, with seven of the spaces left empty. Chlorine has seven electrons in its outer shell, with room for one more.

Elements take part in chemical reactions that make their outer electron shells more stable. An atom can do this by giving away an electron, taking one from another atom, or sharing its electrons with another atom so that they both have full outer shells.

ARRANGING ELECTRONS

Element	Atomic number	Number of electrons in shell 1	shell 2	shell 3	Spaces in outer shell
Hydrogen	1	1			1
Helium	2	2			0
Lithium	3	2	1		7
Carbon	6	2	4		4
Magnesium	12	2	8	2	6
Chlorine	17	2	8	7	1

↑ This table shows the electron arrangement of some elements. Although the number of electrons in the inner shells varies as the atoms get larger, it is the number of electrons in the outer shell that governs how the atom reacts. Atoms with few outer electrons tend to lose them in reactions. Those with a nearly full outer shell form compounds by gaining or sharing electrons.

For example, lithium atoms lose their single outer electron during reactions. As a result, the atom also loses its whole second shell, and its first shell becomes the outer one. This shell has two electrons in it, so it is full and very stable. On the other hand, chlorine atoms gain an electron when they react. This makes them stable by completing their own outer shell.

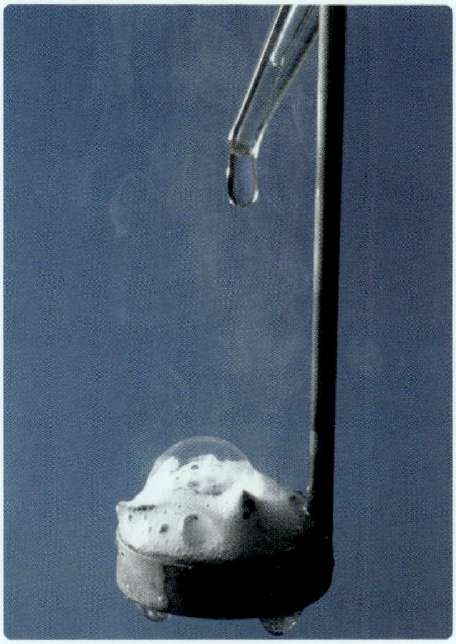

→ Lithium is a reactive metal. It has one electron in its outer shell. It is even more reactive than hydrogen, which also has one electron in its outer shell. When added to water (H_2O), it will displace one of the hydrogen atoms to form lithium hydroxide.

CHAPTER 5

Chemical Bonds and Reactions

Chemical bonding is when two or more atoms or molecules combine to form a different chemical compound. Chemical reactions rearrange the atoms to form new substances that affect all aspects of our daily lives.

A chemical reaction takes place when two or more substances are mixed together in the right conditions. The substances that are the ingredients needed for the reaction are called the reactants. During the reaction, the atoms inside the reactants separate from each other and reorganize. They form into one or more new substances. Scientists call these substances the products.

Reactants may be elements—with just one type of atom in them—or compounds that are made up of different types of atoms. The products may also be either elements or different compounds. During chemical reactions, no atoms are made or destroyed. All that happens is that they are rearranged. The number of atoms in the reactants always remains the same as the number of atoms in the products.

Chemists show what has happened during a chemical reaction with a chemical equation. Chemical equations have two sides. The left-hand side shows the formulas

← One of the most important chemical reactions happens in plants. Plants use energy from the sun to change water and carbon dioxide into sugars and oxygen.

TRY THIS

You can see a quick, safe, and easy chemical reaction for yourself using two common household compounds. Mix a spoonful of baking soda (sodium bicarbonate) with vinegar (ethanoic acid). It is easier to see the results if you use a clear glass or beaker. When the baking soda is added, it begins to fizz. The sodium bicarbonate reacts with the acid to produce three new compounds—water, sodium ethanoate, and carbon dioxide gas. The water and sodium ethanoate form a solution in the glass, while the gas, which causes the fizzing, bubbles away.

← Sodium bicarbonate and ethanoic acid use heat to react, so if you touch the beaker during the reaction, it will feel a little cold.

of the reactants and the number of molecules that are needed for the reaction. The right-hand side shows the formulas of the products and the number of molecules that have been formed.

Coal burning in air is a simple reaction. Coal is mainly pure carbon. The carbon (C) reacts with molecules of oxygen (O_2) in the air. The product of this reaction is carbon dioxide gas (CO_2). The equation for this reaction is:

Carbon + oxygen → carbon dioxide

$$C + O_2 \rightarrow CO_2$$

The reaction between carbon and oxygen releases heat and light. Flames are super-hot carbon and oxygen atoms in the process of reacting. People have burned coal as a fuel for centuries because the reaction it produces gives off so much heat.

Other reactions do not produce heat. Instead, these sorts of reactions need to be heated to make them work. When chalky calcium carbonate ($CaCO_3$) is heated, it breaks up into calcium oxide (CaO) and carbon dioxide (CO_2). However, if the stone is left unheated, the reaction will not take place. The equation for this reaction is:

$$CaCO_3 \rightarrow CaO + CO_2$$

KEY TERMS

Reactants: The ingredients necessary for a chemical reaction.
Products: The new substance or substances that are created during a chemical reaction.

REVOLUTIONARY CHEMIST

Antoine Lavoisier was a political liberal who took part in the historic events that led to the French Revolution. Nevertheless, he was beheaded for being a tax collector.

The brilliant French scientist Antoine Lavoisier (1743–1794) was one of the most important people in modern chemistry. As well as his discovery of the element oxygen, Lavoisier did a lot of work to show that atoms were not made or destroyed by chemical reactions, but simply rearranged themselves to form new compounds. He carried out many experiments in which he carefully weighed the reactants and then all the products. Each time, his results showed that the amount of matter was always the same after a reaction as it had been before it. The principle he proved is called the law of conservation of mass. Lavoisier was a member of a noble family from Paris. He inherited a large fortune from his parents but became even wealthier by collecting taxes from poor French workers. He used his large fortune to pay for his many experiments. However, after the French Revolution in 1789, his money was taken away. Lavoisier was eventually beheaded, along with many other tax collectors.

The Hoover Dam in America was built between 1931 and 1936. Pouring the concrete had to be done carefully to avoid cracking due to the chemical reaction that produces concrete. A lot of heat is produced by the breaking and making of chemical bonds when calcium compounds in cement react with water.

A lime kiln is used to heat chalk, a form of calcium carbonate, to produce a chemical reaction. Heat breaks the bonds in calcium carbonate, turning it into calcium oxide (lime) and carbon dioxide. Lime can be used as a fertilizer and was used to paint buildings white in the past.

Breaking and Forming Bonds

Whether a reaction produces or takes in heat depends on the bonds in the reactants and products. These bonds hold the molecules together. During a chemical reaction, some of the bonds in the reactants are broken, and then new bonds form to make the products.

Energy is needed to break a bond, and energy is released when new bonds are formed. When a reaction has finished, there is usually a difference between the energy used to break bonds and the energy released as new bonds are made. If more energy is released as the new bonds form than was used to break the old ones, then the reaction releases the spare energy as heat and light. If the new bonds release less energy than was used to break the old bonds, then extra energy is needed to make the reaction.

Bonding Process

Atoms can bond in a number of ways. There are three main types of bonds—ionic, covalent, and metallic. The way particular elements form bonds depends on how many electrons their atoms have in their outer shell. Some elements produce stronger bonds than others. Strong bonds need a lot of energy to break them. They are produced when two very reactive atoms bond.

An element's reactivity depends on something called electronegativity. That is a measure of how strongly one atom holds on to its electrons and pulls on the electrons of

Toothpaste commonly contains compounds of fluorine, such as sodium fluoride, which help prevent tooth decay. Fluorine is the most electronegative element, so it is highly reactive. In its elemental form, it is a poisonous gas. When combined with other elements, however, it may have very different properties.

other atoms. Elements that have an outer electron shell with only a few empty spaces left to fill will pull on electrons the most strongly. Nonmetals are the most electronegative. Fluorine gas is the most electronegative element. It has just one space to fill in its outer shell, so it strongly attracts electrons from other atoms. That makes fluorine very likely to react.

Elements with very low electronegativity are also highly reactive. These elements have just a few electrons in their outer shell. Elements like this are generally metals. Metals do not pull electrons toward them and they hold on to their outer electrons very lightly. This makes them electropositive. The most electropositive elements, such as cesium and francium, have only one electron in their outer shell. When they lose this electron, they become stable.

KEY TERMS

Electronegativity is the power of an atom to attract an electron. Nonmetals, which have only a few spaces in their outer shell, are the most electronegative. Metals, which have several empty spaces, are the least electronegative elements. These metals tend to lose electrons in chemical reactions. Metals of this type are termed electropositive.

Fluorine — most electronegative
Oxygen
Chlorine
Nitrogen
Bromine
Iodine
Sulfur

Sodium
Radium
Barium
Potassium
Rubidium
Cesium
Francium — most electropositive

Forming Ionic Bonds

When electronegative and electropositive atoms react, they form ionic bonds. An ion is a charged version of an atom. A positively charged ion is an atom that has lost one or more of its electrons. Atoms that gain electrons become negative ions. The size

IONIC BOND

Sodium chloride is a compound held together by an ionic bond. When an ionic bond forms, the single electron in a sodium atom's outer shell breaks free, leaving behind a full outer shell. The sodium atom becomes a positive sodium ion (Na^+). The free electron moves to the chlorine atom. It takes the final place in that atom's outer shell, making the atom a negative chloride ion (Cl^-). The two ions have opposite charges, so they are attracted to each other. This is the force that bonds them together.

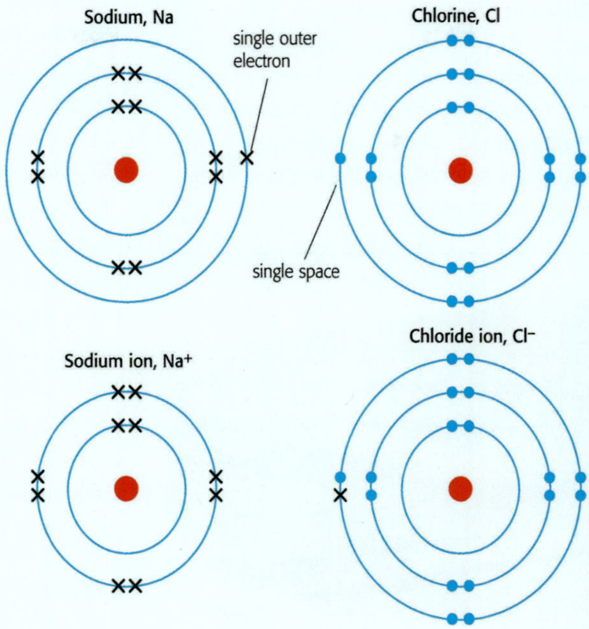

of an ion's charge depends on how many electrons it has lost or gained. For example, chlorine (Cl) atoms gain a single electron to become negative (Cl^-) ions. However, calcium atoms can lose two electrons to become positive (Ca^{2+}) ions.

Charged objects are attracted to objects with an opposite charge. This is the same force that keeps an electron orbiting a nucleus. Ions with opposite charges are pulled toward each other by this force. It is this attraction that holds the two of them together, forming an ionic bond.

Forming Covalent Bonds

Some elements are neither particularly electropositive nor electronegative. That is because the outer shell is more or less half filled. Such elements have just as many electrons to lose as they have to gain to have a full outer shell. For example, carbon atoms have four electrons in their outer shell. To become stable by having a full outer shell, a carbon atom has two options. It can either pull four electrons off other atoms or it can release its four outer electrons. Both are very unlikely because they would require

KEY TERMS

Covalent bond: Bond in which atoms share one or more electrons.
Ionic bond: Bond in which one atom gives one or more electrons to another atom.
Metallic bond: Bond in which outer electrons are free to move in the spaces between the atoms.

huge amounts of energy. Instead, carbon and similar elements get a full outer shell by sharing electrons. The shared electrons sit in the outer shells of both atoms. That is called a covalent bond. Each of the shared electrons is being pulled by the nucleus of both atoms. This is the force that holds the atoms together.

Each covalent bond involves two electrons being shared. Some atoms can form more than one covalent bond at a time. For example, a carbon atom can form four covalent bonds at once. These four bonds can be with four other atoms. Sometimes, however, two atoms share two pairs of electrons. These are called double bonds. Carbon can even form triple bonds, which share three pairs of electrons.

Metallic Bonds

Metals are generally hard solids that can be bent or stretched without breaking. They are also good conductors (carriers) of heat and electricity. These properties are the result of the way in which a metal's atoms are bonded.

The connections between metals' atoms are called metallic bonds. Metallic bonds involve metal atoms sharing some or all of their outer electrons. Nearly all metallic elements

← The atoms in a rubber band are connected in long, coiled molecules. These molecules are connected to each other by covalent bonds. When the rubber band is stretched, the long molecules uncoil until the covalent bonds prevent further stretching. Any further tension on the band causes these covalent bonds to break and the band snaps.

SHARING ELECTRONS

Nonmetals tend to form covalent bonds with each other. Many nonmetal atoms combine with atoms of the same element to form simple molecules using these bonds. For example, oxygen forms O_2 and fluorine forms F_2. Carbon forms bonds with hydrogen to form methane. By sharing electrons in a covalent bond, the elements form molecules that are more stable than atoms on their own.

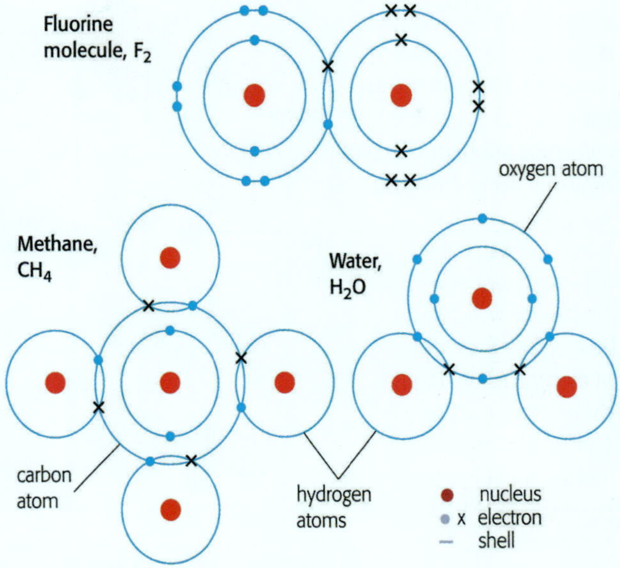

have only one or two outer electrons. Only a few metals, such as lead, bismuth, and tin, have more. When a metal's atoms are packed closely together, as in a solid or liquid, the outer electrons from each atom break free. The free electrons form a "sea" of electrons that can move around and are shared by all the atoms. The positively charged nucleus inside a metal atom is attracted to the negatively charged electron sea all around it. This force holds metal atoms in place.

← The Eiffel Tower, once the world's tallest structure, is made from iron. Iron is strong enough to support such a tall structure because of its close metallic bonds.

ELECTRON SEA

Within a metal, nuclei are attracted in all directions to the "sea" of electrons that surrounds them, so the nuclei and electrons are held together very strongly. Because the sea of electrons can move, it carries heat and electricity well. (Electricity is a flow of electrons moving through a substance.) That is why most metals are very good conductors of heat and electricity.

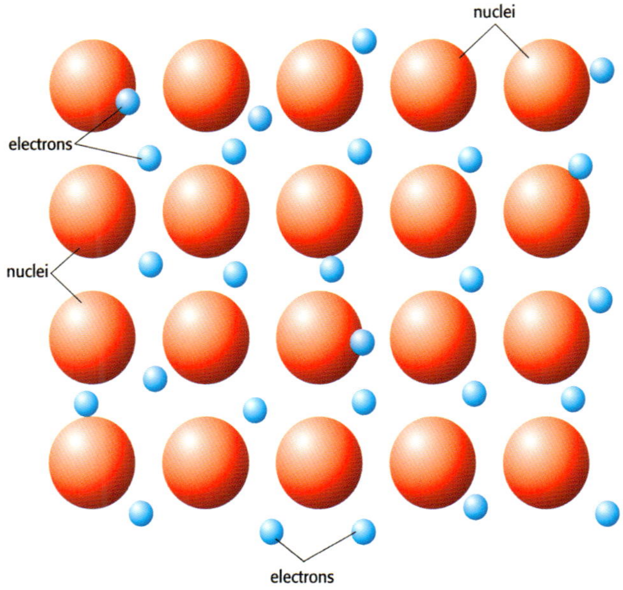

Van Der Waals Forces

Ionic, covalent, and metallic bonds hold atoms together. However, there are other forces that also make atoms and molecules cling together. Most of these are very weak. For example, tiny temporary forces are produced by the random movement of the electrons. The electrons in an atom or molecule are generally spread out evenly. However, they are all constantly moving and by pure chance they can sometimes all gather in one place at the same time. This gives one end of an atom or molecule a negative charge, and the other end becomes positive. These charges exist for only a very short time, but they have an effect by pushing and pulling on the atoms around them. These forces are named van der Waals forces.

← Copper is often used in electrical wiring because it is a good conductor of electricity. The electrical current is carried by the "sea" of electrons that surrounds the atomic nuclei.

A gecko is a lizard that can cling to surfaces using van der Waals forces. These forces occur between a surface and tiny hairs on the gecko's feet.

Johannes van der Waals (1837–1923) was a Dutch physicist. He was the first scientist to realize the importance of these forces and how they affect the behavior of gases and liquids. Larger molecules produce stronger van der Waals forces than smaller ones. This increases the melting and boiling points of the larger molecules. Even though they are tiny, the van der Waals forces hold molecules together and make it harder to break the bonds between them.

Molecular Dipoles

Some types of molecules always have charged ends. These charged regions are called dipoles. Dipoles are produced when one atom in a molecule is more electronegative than the others. As a result, all the outer electrons in the molecule are drawn toward that atom. Because more of the electrons are at one end, that end, or pole, is negative. The other pole is positive. The charged poles are attracted to the oppositely charged pole of a nearby molecule. Dipoles attract the molecules to one another and make them arrange themselves in a repeating pattern, where the oppositely charged poles are next to each other.

Bonding Hydrogen

Hydrogen bonds are an example of a dipole attraction. As their name suggests, these bonds always involve an atom of hydrogen. When hydrogen is bonded to highly electronegative elements, such as fluorine, oxygen, and nitrogen, it often forms a positive pole. The hydrogen atom's only electron is pulled away by the other atom, leaving just the hydrogen's nucleus. This nucleus is a single proton and has a strong positive charge.

Water is an example of a compound that produces hydrogen bonds. The oxygen atom in the water molecule pulls the electrons from the hydrogen atoms.

The oxygen has a slightly negative charge, and each hydrogen is slightly positive. The positive hydrogen atoms are attracted to the negative pole of another water molecule.

The hydrogen bonds in water ensure that it is a liquid in the normal conditions found on Earth's surface. Without these bonds, water molecules would not be so strongly bonded to each other. As a result, the boiling point of water would be a much lower temperature, and water would be a gas in normal conditions.

KEY TERMS

Dipole attraction: The attractive force between charged ends of molecules.
Hydrogen bond: Dipole attraction that always involves a hydrogen atom.
Intermolecular bonds: The bonds that attract molecules to one another. These bonds are weaker than those between atoms in a molecule.
Van der Waals forces: Short-lived forces between atoms and molecules.

Molecular Shapes

As well as sometimes creating weak forces between molecules, the position of electrons in a molecule has an effect on its shape. Opposite charges attract and like charges repel each other. The electrons in a molecule repel each other, and they tend to stay as far apart as possible. Electrons in an atom's outer shell will repel each other with equal force. However, an electron shared with another atom to form a bond cannot push the other electrons away as strongly. As a result, pairs of shared electrons are often pushed away from the other, unbonded electrons.

The uneven distribution of outer electrons has an effect on the shape of a molecule.

OPPOSITES ATTRACT

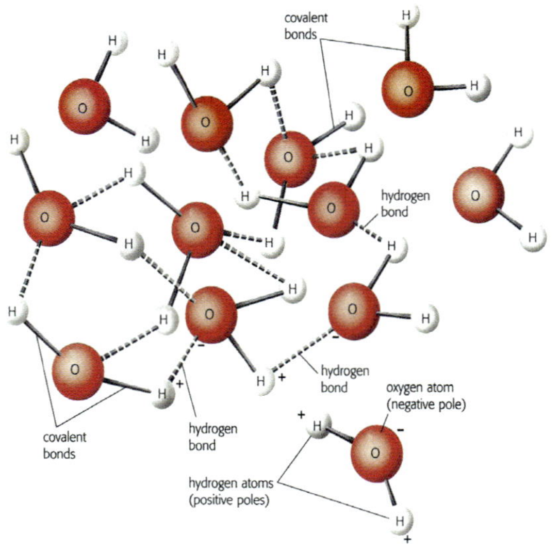

Water (H_2O) molecules form hydrogen bonds. The hydrogen atoms in water have a slight positive charge and the oxygen atoms have a slight negative charge, owing to the arrangement of electrons around each nucleus. These opposite charges attract each other and hold the water molecules loosely together.

FLOATING ICE

Water is an unusual substance. Most substances contract a little when they freeze, but water expands when it turns to ice. As a result, ice is less dense than water. This ensures that ponds and rivers always freeze from the top down and makes it possible for huge icebergs to float in the ocean. Ice takes up more room than water because of hydrogen bonds. As water freezes, these bonds force the molecules into a widely spaced crystal structure. When ice melts, hydrogen bonds have less of an effect, the bonds continually break and reform, and the molecules mingle more closely with each other, taking up less room.

A molecule with two atoms, such as a chlorine gas molecule (Cl_2), always forms a straight line and can be thought of as a miniature dumbbell. However, when a molecule has more than one bond in it, the shape can be more complicated.

A molecule of methane gas contains one carbon atom at its center. There are four hydrogen atoms bonded to the carbon. Carbon has four electrons, and each one makes a covalent bond with one of the hydrogens. Therefore all pairs of electrons are identical and they all repel each other equally. The result of this is that methane molecules form a tetrahedron—a type of pyramid.

However, water molecules are shaped by the force of unbonded electrons. Each molecule is made up of two hydrogen atoms joined to a single oxygen atom by covalent bonds. The molecule is not straight but bent, with both the hydrogen atoms being on the same side of the oxygen atom. That is because the two pairs of shared electrons in the molecule's bonds are being repelled by the oxygen atom's six other electrons.

Atoms can also form molecules with complex shapes. Carbon atoms can join to make spherical molecules of connected hexagons and pentagons. These molecules are called buckminsterfullerenes after the American engineer and inventor Buckminster Fuller (1895–1983). Fuller designed domes that have the same structure as these carbon molecules. Carbon can also form sheets of hexagons that roll up to form hollow tubes.

There is often a smell of rotten eggs around hot springs. This is caused by hydrogen sulfide (H_2S), which has a molecular shape similar to that of water.

SHAPES OF MOLECULES

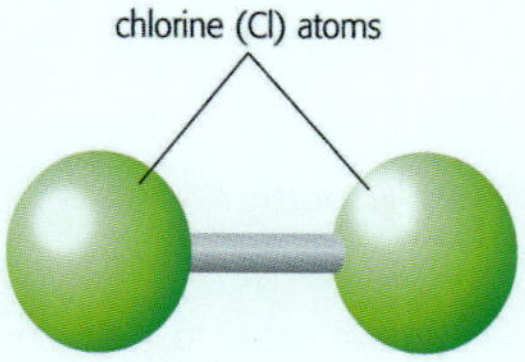

A chlorine gas molecule (Cl_2) forms a dumbbell shape.

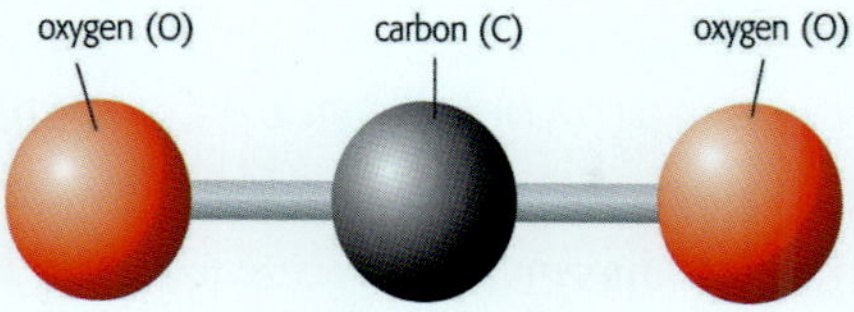

In carbon dioxide (CO_2), the atoms form a straight line.

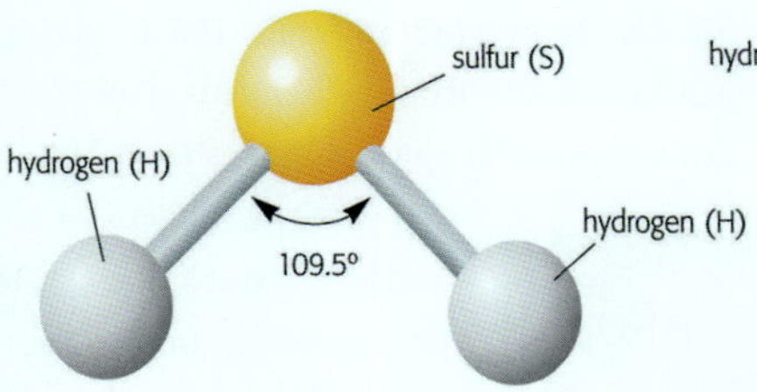

Hydrogen sulfide (H_2S) has an angle of 109.5° between the hydrogen and sulfur atoms. Hydrogen sulfide has a similar molecular shape to water (H_2O), which has a bond angle of 104°.

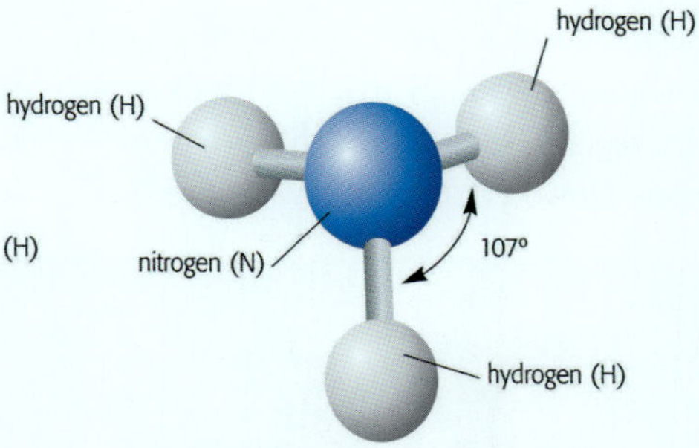

An ammonia (NH_3) molecule has the shape of a flattened pyramid. The angle between any two of the hydrogen atoms and the nitrogen atom is 107°.

Methane (CH_4) forms a pyramid with a single carbon atom at its center. The angle between any two hydrogen atoms and the carbon atom is 109.5°.

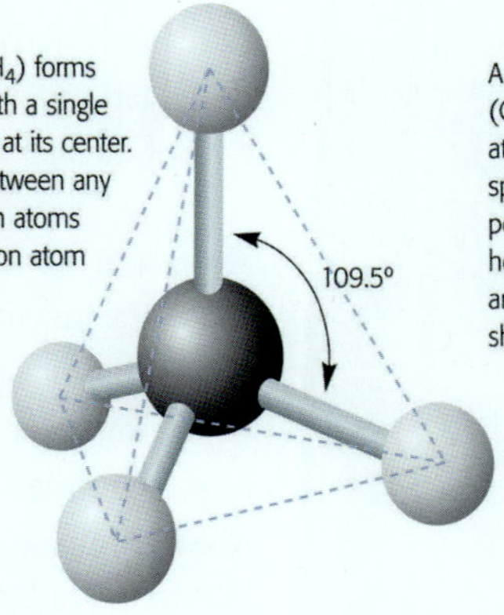

A buckminsterfullerene (C_{60}) has 60 carbon atoms arranged in a sphere made of pentagons and hexagons (five- and six-sided shapes).

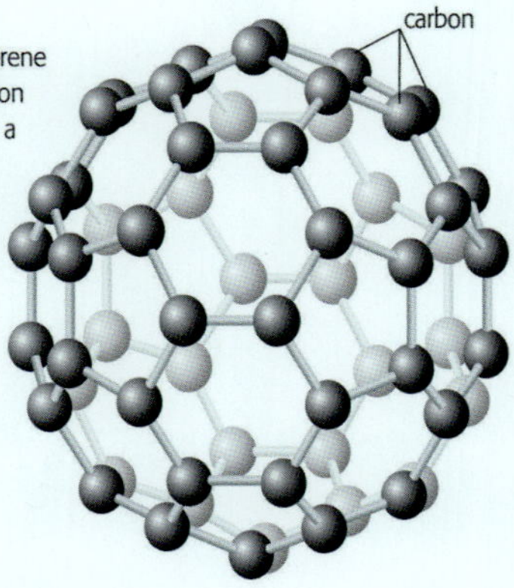

CHAPTER 6

Radioactivity

By the end of the 19th century, scientists understood much about atomic structure. Then came a significant discovery. Some elements are unstable and their atoms break apart. This releases energy in a process scientists named radioactivity.

An atom is described as being radioactive if it has an unstable nucleus. An atom's nucleus is made of positively charged protons and neutral neutrons. Particles with the same charge repel each other, and that is true of protons. However, the protons stay together in the nucleus instead of being forced apart. That happens because there is an even stronger attractive force that bonds the protons and neutrons in place. Radioactivity occurs when this strong force cannot keep the nucleus together.

Inside the nucleus of a radioactive atom, the ratio of protons to neutrons makes it hard for the strong force to hold the particles together. Eventually, small amounts of the nucleus break off and escape from the atom. This process is called radioactive decay. Radioactive decay is a type of nuclear reaction.

← Atom bombs make use of the instability of radioactive elements. By exploding these elements, huge quantities of energy are released, along with invisible but deadly radiation.

➔ These crystals contain uranium, one of the most common radioactive elements. The crystals are processed to produce uranium metal pellets, which are used to fuel nuclear power plants.

Nuclear reactions are different than chemical reactions. Chemical reactions involve just the electrons in an atom. Nuclear reactions result in changes to the nucleus of an atom.

Radioactive Elements

Radioactive elements are usually elements with very large atoms. Their atoms have so many particles in each nucleus that they are more unstable than smaller atoms. For example, uranium atoms have between 234 and 238 particles in their nucleus. Uranium is one of the most common radioactive elements. There are nine other naturally occurring elements with atoms that are always radioactive: bismuth, polonium, astatine, radon, francium, radium, actinium, thorium, and protactinium.

However, some isotopes of other elements are radioactive. Isotopes are atoms that have the same atomic number but have a different atomic mass. One of the rare hydrogen

RADIATION TYPES

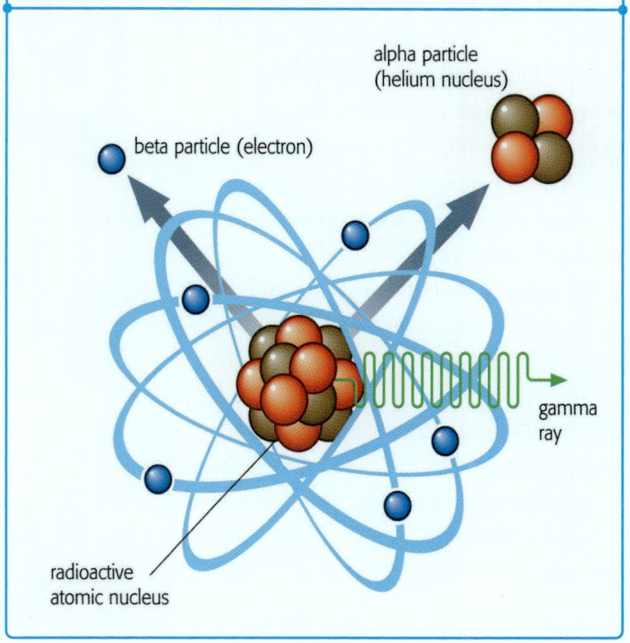

ANTIMATTER

A few beta particles have a positive charge. They are the same size as electrons but have an equal and opposite charge. Particles like this are called positrons. Scientists describe particles such as positrons as antimatter. Each one is exactly the same as a particle of matter—in this case, an electron —but has an opposite charge. When matter and antimatter particles meet, they are destroyed completely, releasing gamma rays. Positron beta particles are produced when a proton in a nucleus turns into a neutron.

isotopes—tritium—is radioactive. Radioactive isotopes are known as radioisotopes. Radioisotopes are always less common than the stable version of an element. For example, one in every trillion carbon atoms is the radioisotope carbon-14. All the others are stable carbon-12.

Three Kinds of Radiation

Radioactivity produces three types of radiation. These are alpha particles, beta particles, and gamma rays. (Alpha, beta, and gamma are the first three letters in the Greek alphabet.) Most nuclear reactions release either an alpha particle or a beta particle. All nuclear reactions produce gamma rays.

Alpha particles are two protons and two neutrons stuck together. This is the same as the nucleus of a helium atom, so alpha particles are often written as ${}^{4}_{2}He^{2+}$. The 4 refers to the atomic mass of the nucleus (how heavy it is) and the 2 refers to the atomic number (the number of protons) of the atom. Because alpha particles do not have any electrons attached to them, the protons they contain give them a positive charge.

People who work with radioactive substances put up signs to warn of the dangers because radiation cannot be seen, smelled, or felt. This sign shows that there are radioactive materials nearby.

Most beta particles are fast-moving electrons. They have a negative charge just like the electrons that orbit atoms. Beta particles are produced when a neutron in an unstable nucleus breaks down into a proton. A proton is slightly smaller than a neutron, and the leftover matter flies away in the form of an electron.

Gamma rays are energy waves that belong to the electromagnetic spectrum. This spectrum includes light, heat, radio waves, and X-rays. Gamma rays contain more energy than any other type of wave. Some nuclear reactions also produce X-rays.

KEY TERMS

Electromagnetic spectrum: The range of energy waves that includes light, heat, and radio waves.
Ionization: The formation of ions by adding or removing electrons from atoms.
Isotopes: Atoms with the same atomic number but a different atomic mass due to varying numbers of neutrons.
Radiation: The products of radioactivity—alpha and beta particles and gamma rays.

STOPPING RADIOACTIVE PARTICLES

Radioactive particles have different powers of penetration. An alpha particle is relatively large and is easily stopped by a sheet of paper. Beta particles are smaller and faster. It takes a sheet of aluminum 1/5-inch (5 mm) thick to stop them. Gamma rays are difficult to stop—a lead sheet at least 4/5-inch (2 cm) thick is needed.

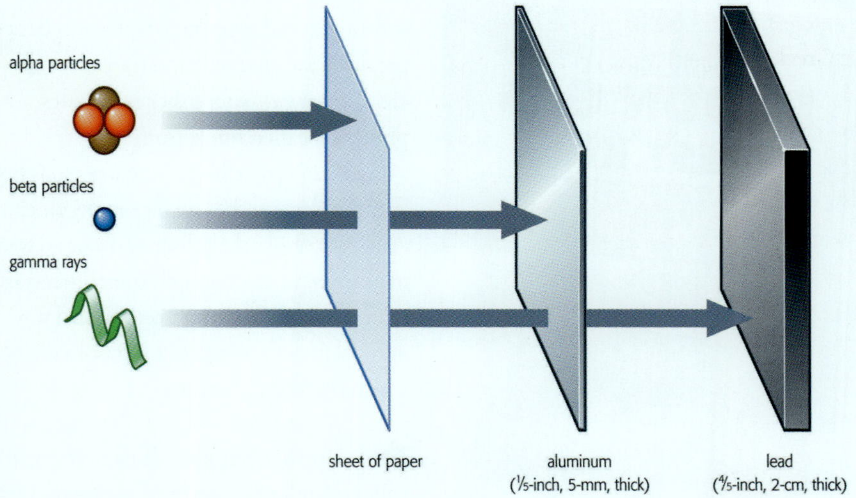

NUCLEAR TRANSFORMATION

Radioactive elements can undergo any of three types of decay. These types are alpha, beta, and gamma. Often the type of decay varies with each stage of the process. The atomic number and mass number of the element both change with alpha and beta decay, as these involve the loss of protons or neutrons, but stay the same when gamma rays are given off.

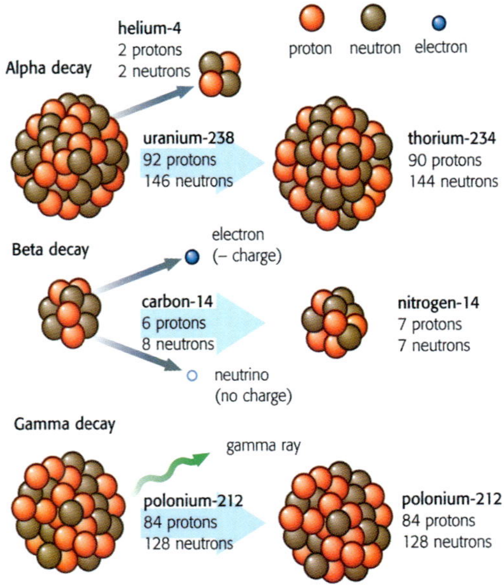

Hazardous Radiation

All radiation produced by radioactive substances is dangerous. Alpha and beta particles are charged, and they can rip electrons away from other molecules. This process is called ionization.

If radiation particles get into a person's body, they can damage the complex molecules inside cells. As a result, the cells may die or go wrong in other ways. For example, sometimes cells go wrong by growing in an uncontrolled way. This unusual growth produces a tumor in the body, which is a type of cancer.

← Radon is a natural radioactive gas that collects under houses in some areas. Testing kits are available to detect its presence.

Alpha particles are the largest type of radiation and cause the most damage. They are easy to stop, however, because they cannot pass easily through solid objects. They can be blocked by a sheet of paper or clothing.

Beta particles are much smaller than alpha particles, so they can penetrate farther into solid objects. However, once they are inside the body, they do less damage than alpha particles because they are so small. Beta particles can be blocked by a thin sheet of metal.

Gamma rays cause ionization inside the body. They are more penetrating than alpha particles or beta particles. Gamma rays can pass through clothing, metal sheets, and most other everyday objects. Only thick slabs of lead will stop them completely. However, only a fraction of the gamma rays are absorbed by body tissues. Many pass right through the body without having any effect.

Becoming a New Element

After a nucleus has decayed, the number of protons it contains changes. If the nuclear reaction released an alpha particle, there are two fewer protons in the nucleus. If the reaction released a beta particle, one neutron changed into a proton. The nucleus now

URANIUM-238 DECAY CHAIN

The radioactive decay chain for uranium-238 takes 14 steps before one atom of uranium is finally converted into a stable isotope of lead.

Radiation emitted alpha (α) or beta (β)	Isotope	Half-life
	uranium-238	4.5 billion years (4.5×10^9)
α		
	thorium-234	24.5 days
β		
	protactinium-234	1.14 minutes
β		
	uranium-234	233,000 years (2.33×10^5)
α		
	thorium-230	83,000 years (8.3×10^4)
α		
	radium-226	1,590 years
α		
	radon-222	3.825 days
α		
	polonium-218	3.05 minutes
α		
	lead-214	26.8 minutes
β		
	bismuth-214	19.7 minutes
β		
	polonium-214	0.00015 seconds (1.5×10^{-4})
α		
	lead-210	22 years
β		
	bismuth-210	5 days
β		
	polonium-210	140 days
α		
	lead-206	stable

MARIE AND PIERRE CURIE

Polish physicist Marie Curie (1867–1934) and her French husband Pierre (1859–1906) were pioneers in the study of radioactivity. They even coined the term radioactivity to describe what they were investigating. Although radiation in the form of X-rays was already known by the time the Curies began work in 1898, nobody really knew where it came from. Henri Bequerel (1852–1908) had already shown that uranium ores gave off radiation. The Curies discovered that the strength of radiation emitted by a uranium ore depended on the amount of uranium atoms in the compound. The Curies also noticed that a mineral called pitchblende contained uranium compounds that produced more radiation than they expected. They realized the rock must contain other radioactive elements. They identified two of these.

The two new elements were named polonium (for Marie's home country Poland) and radium. The Curies received the 1903 Nobel Prize in Physics for their work. Marie Curie also won the 1911 Nobel Prize in Chemistry for her discovery of radium and polonium.

← This cartoon from the British magazine *Vanity Fair* shows Marie and Pierre Curie in their laboratory. Their discovery of two new elements brought them international fame and attracted wide interest in their work.

has one more proton than it had before. In both cases, the reactions change the atom's atomic number and it becomes a new element.

For example, an atom of the most common uranium isotope, U-238, which has the atomic number 92, releases an alpha particle as it decays. It loses two protons and turns into an atom of thorium. That element has the atomic number 90. Thorium is also radioactive. When the thorium atom decays, it releases a beta particle. As a result of that type of decay, the atom's nucleus loses a neutron but gains a proton. That gives it a new atomic number of 91, and the atom has become protactinium.

Decay Chains

In the example of uranium's radioactive decay, one radioactive atom decays into another. It may take many nuclear reactions before an atom decays into a stable element and all radioactive behavior comes to an end.

Several different elements are produced by the string of nuclear reactions. This is called the decay chain. For example, the decay chain of uranium-238 contains a total of 14 other isotopes. The chain eventually ends when stable lead-206 atoms are produced.

The most common naturally occurring radioactive elements on Earth are thorium and uranium. They are found in rocks throughout the world. Most of the other radioactive substances that occur are produced as part of the decay chains of more common elements.

The rarer radioactive elements include radon, which is the only radioactive element that is a gas, and francium, which is the most reactive (and rarest) of all metals. The rare elements are more unstable than thorium and uranium and break down quickly.

DECAY CURVE

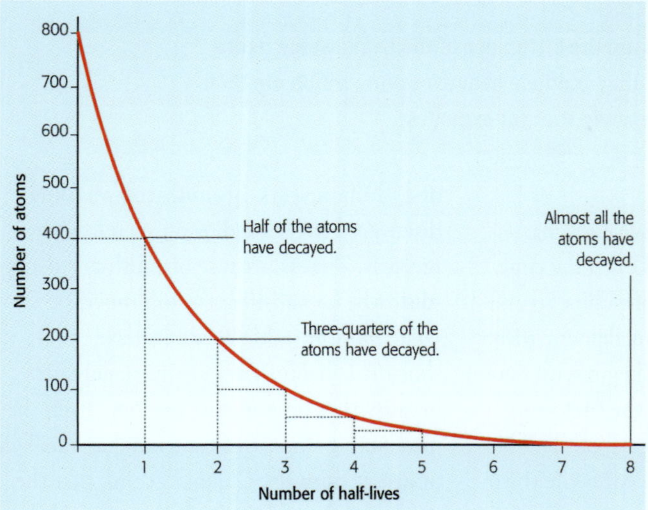

All radioactive elements decay at a constant rate called a half-life. The half-life of each radioactive element is different. Whatever the period of the half-life is, the same curve results when plotted on a graph. The quantity of the element reduces by half by the end of each half-life, until it reaches zero and the element stabilizes.

↑ A graph of the decay of a radioactive element takes the shape of a decreasing curve. The example above shows how 800 atoms of an element with a half-life of 1 year reduces in quantity. At the end of the first year, 400 atoms are left. After 8 years (8 half-lives), only about one atom of the original radioactive element remains.

Supernovas such as this are the birthplace of the heaviest elements. As giant stars run out of fuel, they produce heavier atoms, which are then flung into the wider universe when the star explodes.

Decay Rates

The rate at which a radioactive element decays is called its half-life. This is the time it takes for half of a sample of radioactive elements to decay. Imagine an element with a half-life of one year. Let us begin with 800 atoms of this element. After the first year, only 400 are left. Over the next year, half of the atoms decay, leaving 200. After the third year, 100 atoms remain. This continues until there are no atoms of the element left.

Common radioisotopes are relatively stable and have a very long half-life. For example, thorium-232 has a half-life of 14 billion years. Uranium-238 is less stable but has a half-life of 4.5 billion years. Bismuth-209 was only discovered to be a radioisotope relatively recently. That is because bismuth-209 decays so slowly. Its half-life is 19 billion years.

The most unstable elements have the shortest half-life. They are extremely rare because they do not exist for long. Even the most stable isotope of francium has a half-life of just 22 minutes. Chemists think that the total amount of francium on Earth adds up to less than 1 ounce (28 grams) at any one point in time. Some isotopes are even more unstable and have a half-life of millionths of a second. These isotopes keep undergoing radioactive decay until they reach a state in

ARTIFICIAL ELEMENTS

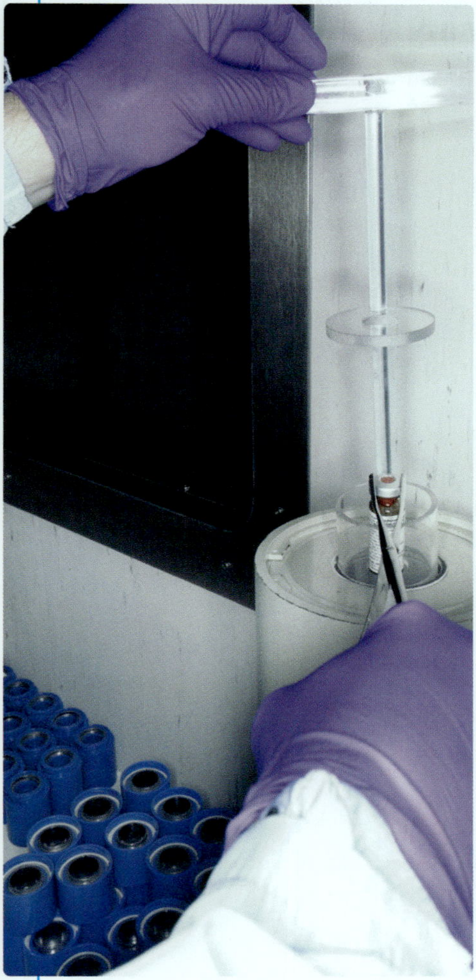

There are around 90 naturally occurring elements, 15 of which are radioactive. In addition, some elements, such as carbon, have radioactive isotopes. Scientists have also made artificial elements, all of which are radioactive. They do this by bombarding large natural elements with smaller ions. The atoms are bombarded at such high speed that the ions merge with them into huge artificial atoms.

Most artificial elements are heavier than uranium. Twenty-six artificial elements have been made so far. Many have been named for famous scientists and include curium (atomic number 96), einsteinium (99), and bohrium (107). Seaborgium (106) was named for American Glenn Seaborg (1912–1999). Seaborg helped make a number of new elements, including plutonium (94), americium (95), berkelium (97), californium (98), and mendelevium (101). These elements all have a very short half-life. For example, the half-life of bohrium is just 10 seconds.

← Nitrogen-13 is an artificial radioisotope with a half-life of 10 minutes. It has to be made just before it is used in a hospital scanner.

which they become stable.

Nuclear Fission

Radioactive decay is not the only type of nuclear reaction. For example, a process called nuclear fission is what powers nuclear power plants and causes nuclear bombs to explode. Another phrase for fission is "splitting the atom." Fission occurs when a neutron is fired at certain radioisotopes, generally uranium-235. The neutron causes the uranium atom to split in two, producing two smaller atoms and a great deal of heat. Each fission also releases more neutrons, which can cause further fissions in neighboring U-235 atoms. Nuclear reactors are used to keep this chain-reaction process under control. However, in nuclear bombs, the chain reaction is allowed to occur at full speed. Huge amounts of energy are released in a devastating explosion.

Fusion

Another type of nuclear reaction is called fusion. This is the opposite of fission. Fusion involves two small atoms being squeezed together to form a larger one. It takes a large force to fuse atoms together, but when they fuse, a huge amount of energy is also released.

Fusion is the reaction that powers the sun. The sun is a ball of hot gas. At its center, atoms are being pushed together with such force that they fuse. In most cases, hydrogen atoms fuse to make helium atoms. This process produces the sun's heat and light.

Fusion is the process by which the many different elements found in nature were created. In the largest stars, where there is enough force pushing into the center, larger atoms form by the fusion process. Atoms up to the size of iron are produced in this way.

The fusion reactions needed to produce the heaviest elements, such as gold and uranium, require gargantuan amounts of energy. Fusion reactions such as these are only possible inside supernovas. Supernovas are caused by the most giant stars running out of the fuel they need to keep shining. The pressure inside a supernova is so high that it can cause even heavy atoms to fuse. The atoms fused inside the explosion are flung into space, where they form clouds of dust and gas.

Over billions of years, the dust gradually clumps together to form a new star. The leftover dust forms planets that orbit the star. Earth was formed by this process about 4.6 billion years ago. Everything we see around us was once part of a star.

CHAPTER 7

BIOGRAPHY

Niels Bohr and Werner Heisenberg

During the 1920s, Bohr and Heisenberg caused a revolution in the world of physics with their research into quantum mechanics.

Niels Bohr was born into a family of great scientific distinction. His father, Christian (1855–1911), was a professor of physiology at Copenhagen University, Denmark, and his younger brother Harald was a distinguished mathematician. Bohr's son, Aage, carried on the family tradition and shared the Nobel Prize in Physics in 1975 for his work on the shape of certain atomic nuclei.

Bohr earned his doctorate from Copenhagen University in 1911 for a paper on the behavior of electrons in metals. That same year, he took up a research post at the University of Manchester, England, joining a team headed by the physicist Ernest Rutherford that was carrying out detailed studies of the structure of the atom.

Models of the Atom

When English scientist John Dalton devised his theory of the atom in the early 19th century, he thought of it as a tiny, solid particle. By the beginning of the 20th century, a new picture of the atom was emerging. Rutherford showed that it contained a heavy, positively charged nucleus, around which much lighter, negatively charged electrons orbited. Because he pictured electrons moving in much the same way the planets orbit the sun in our universe, Rutherford's model became known as the "planetary" model of the atom.

There was a difference between atoms and planets, however. The force that keeps the planets orbiting the sun is gravity, whereas the electrons moving around an atomic nucleus are electrically charged.

According to the rules of physics, accelerating electrically charged particles radiate energy, causing them to slow down. This loss of energy should cause orbiting electrons to collapse extremely rapidly into the central nucleus of the atom. This was obviously not happening, and it led a number of people to question the accuracy of Rutherford's model.

Niels Bohr turned to the description of light put forward by German physicist Max Planck in 1900 to see if that would explain the behavior of electrons. Planck had stated that light is emitted in separate packets, or "quanta," also known as photons. This was the beginning of "quantum theory," which revolutionized physics in the early 20th century. Planck discovered that the energy of the photons equals their frequency multiplied by an incredibly small number known as Planck's constant (*h*).

Using Planck's quantum theory as a basis for his observations, Bohr declared that in certain orbits, electrons are stable: They neither lose nor gain energy as they race around. The momentum (mass multiplied

Niels Bohr photographed in the early 1940s with a colleague in the laboratory at the Institute for Theoretical Physics in Copenhagen, which he founded in 1918. Bohr made a vital contribution to the understanding of the structure of the atom and of nuclear fission.

by speed) of an electron in a stable orbit is always a whole-number multiple of Planck's constant *h*: *1h*, *2h*, *3h*, and so on. According to the Bohr model of the atom, then, the orbiting electrons are limited to a series of possible orbits. Energy is radiated or absorbed—lost or gained—only when electrons jump between orbits, either to a higher-energy orbit or to a lower one. When an electron moves from a higher to a lower-energy state, it emits a photon of equal energy to the difference between the energies of the two states. When an electron moves from a lower to a higher state, it absorbs a photon, which has the same energy as the difference between the energies of the two states. Bohr's argument, described in his 1913 paper "On the Constitution of Atoms and Molecules," showed why Rutherford's model of the atom was fundamentally correct, and provided scientists with a convincing explanation as to why the atom was stable rather than unstable.

When elements are heated, they give off light that covers a specific range of frequencies or wavelengths and is therefore of a particular color. This is known as a spectrum. So, for example, the yellow light given off by sodium streetlights is the specific set of frequencies of the element sodium.

PHOTONS

A diagram of an atom shows electrons orbiting its nucleus. An atom emits or absorbs light in discrete packets called photons. If an electron absorbs a photon, it moves from an orbit nearer the nucleus to one farther away. If it emits a photon, it moves back from a more distant orbit to one closer to the nucleus.

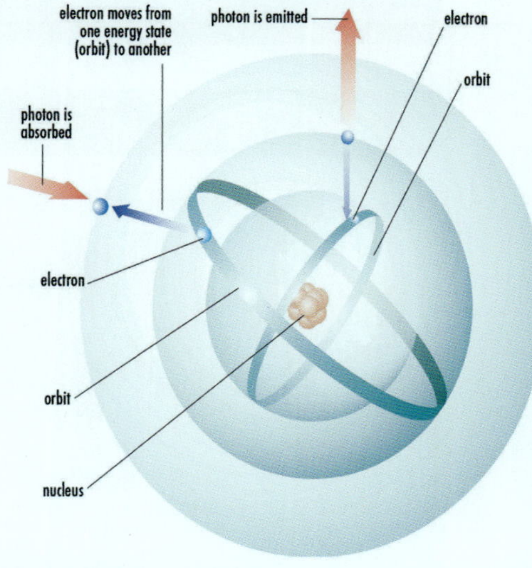

A spectroscopist examines a spectrum of light in the 19th century. Absorption spectra are shown above and below in this vignette.

SPECTOGRAPH

This diagram shows how a spectograph works. Light passes through a narrow entrance slit and is formed into parallel rays by a lens.

These are refracted by a prism, and a second lens refocuses the light rays onto a photographic plate, where the spectral lines appear.

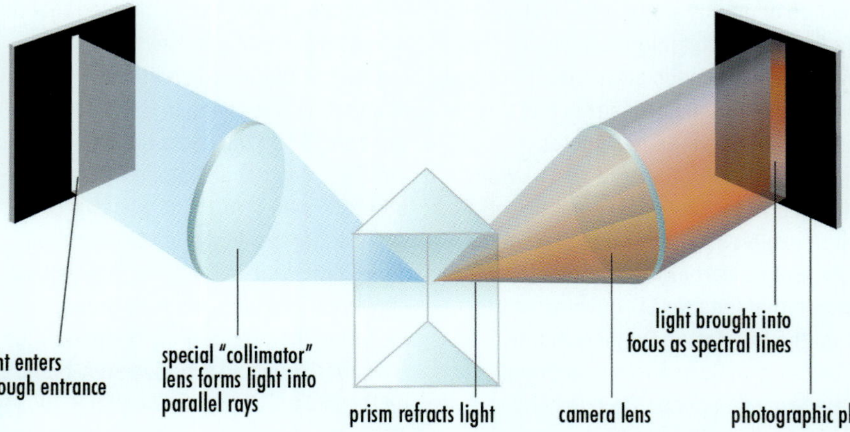

Emission Spectrum of Hydrogen

Other elements emit light of a different set of frequencies. Frequencies can be used almost like fingerprints, allowing elements to be identified by the light they emit. Bohr's 1913 account of the atom was tested against—and partly inspired by—the spectrum of the hydrogen atom.

When hydrogen is heated and its light is passed through a prism—a transparent triangular solid used to refract light—its spectrum consists of a series of colored lines called spectral lines. Each line represents light of a particular wavelength. Bohr realized that the lines in the hydrogen spectrum were caused by electrons jumping between higher- and lower-energy orbits.

When the electrons jump, they emit a photon of light of a particular frequency, which appears as a line. All gases, when heated, produce spectral lines.

Bohr and the Atom Bomb

In 1918, Bohr was chosen to head up a new Institute for Theoretical Physics in Copenhagen, and in 1922, he was awarded the Nobel Prize in Physics for his work on atomic theory. Over the next 20 years, the Institute became the world center for the new quantum physics, attracting scientists from many countries. Bohr himself traveled extensively on lecture tours in Europe, Canada, and the United States.

In April 1940, German troops invaded and occupied Denmark. Bohr, who was

GERMANY AND THE A-BOMB

In 1938, German scientists Otto Hahn and Lise Meitner found a way of splitting the nuclei of uranium atoms, called nuclear fission. Nuclear fission releases massive amounts of energy, and it was clear to some people that it might be used to create weapons of enormous power. Bohr brought news of what Hahn and Meitner had done when he visited the United States in January 1939. With the outbreak of World War II, fears that Germany might be the first to exploit nuclear fission grew more acute. Bohr's warning helped fuel the concern that led the U.S. government to set up the Manhattan Project. Meanwhile Heisenberg, in Germany, was ordered by the Army Weapons Office to head a project to see if an atomic bomb (A-bomb) could be created.

In 1941, Heisenberg called on Bohr in Copenhagen. There has been much controversy about why he made this visit. Bohr had of course been Heisenberg's mentor at the Institute for Theoretical Physics in Copenhagen in the 1920s; however, since April 1940, Denmark had been occupied by German troops. Heisenberg was now a representative of a conquering power. Some people think Heisenberg wanted to find out how close the United States was to developing nuclear weapons; others believe he came to warn Bohr about German progress. Heisenberg himself later claimed that he would have sabotaged any attempt by German scientists to create an A-bomb, and that he was trying to suggest that Bohr should do the same on the Allied side.

In 1945, Heisenberg, along with nine other German scientists, was captured by Allied forces and taken to Farm Hall, near Cambridge in England. The group's conversations were secretly taped, including their reaction to the news that the Americans had dropped an A-bomb on Hiroshima, Japan, on August 6, 1945. The Farm Hall tapes seem to confirm that German scientists never really had a clear idea of how to develop a fission weapon; time and again Heisenberg is heard to exclaim, "I don't believe a word about the bomb." As the American Manhattan Project showed, nothing less than an all-out program using every available resource was needed to produce a viable atomic weapon. It now seems clear that in war-pressed Germany, these resources were simply not available.

of Jewish descent, did not conceal his anti-Nazi sympathies. He struggled to keep the Institute going, but in September 1943, he was warned that he was about to be arrested by the Nazis and fled to safety in Sweden. By December, Bohr was in the United States working on the Manhattan atom bomb project at Los Alamos, New Mexico. However, he was increasingly concerned about the dangers of nuclear weapons and was convinced that the best way of controlling them was by the free exchange of knowledge between scientists and governments. After World War II, he

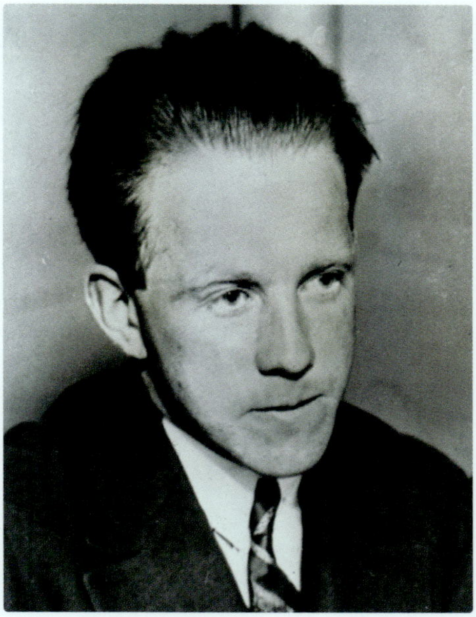

Werner Karl Heisenberg was a lecturer in theoretical physics at the University of Copenhagen in 1926. When he was only 26 years old, he became a professor at the University of Leipzig.

campaigned for the peaceful use of nuclear energy and cofounded the European Center for Nuclear Research (CERN). He died in Copenhagen in 1962.

Heisenberg

Sixteen years younger than Bohr, Werner Heisenberg was born in Würzburg, Germany. He studied physics at the University of Munich and Göttingen University, where he earned his doctorate in 1923. The following year, he traveled to Copenhagen and worked for two years with Bohr at the Institute for Theoretical Physics. In 1927, he was appointed professor of theoretical physics at the University of Leipzig in Germany.

Faced with many conflicting ideas that were emerging about quantum theory, Heisenberg was determined to construct a mathematical system that would explain the structure of the atom. He believed it was a mistake to think of the atom in visual terms, like the planetary model that Rutherford had described. Heisenberg only wanted to deal with what could be established by experiment. What could be observed about the hydrogen atom was its spectrum. He began to write down the differences between the observed frequencies in the hydrogen spectrum and arranged them as a set of figures in a square pattern. He found that he could construct equations that gave the

KEY DATES

1885 Bohr born in Copenhagen, Denmark, on October 7
1901 Heisenberg born in Würzburg, Germany, on December 5
1911 Bohr begins working with Rutherford at Manchester University
1913 Bohr proposes a new atomic model
1922 Bohr is awarded Nobel Prize in Physics
1924–1926 Heisenberg works with Bohr in Copenhagen
1927 Heisenberg proposes his uncertainty principle
1932 Heisenberg is awarded Nobel Prize in Physics
1939–1945 Heisenberg directs German atomic bomb program
1943 Bohr flees Nazi-occupied Denmark
1962 Bohr dies on November 18
1976 Heisenberg dies on February 2

frequencies and other observed properties of the spectral lines. However, he ran into a serious difficulty. We know that if we add or multiply two numbers, the order in which we add or multiply the numbers does not matter. For example, $7 \times 8 = 56$, as does 8×7. Mathematicians say that such operations "commute" or are "commutative." However, Heisenberg found that some of his quantum states did not commute: that $p \times q$, for example, did not equal $q \times p$.

Physicist Max Born provided a solution to his problem. Born was then a professor of physics at Göttingen University. He drew Heisenberg's attention to a branch of mathematics that was less well known in the 1920s than it is today. This was matrix mathematics. A matrix (plural: matrices) is the mathematical term for arrays of numbers set out in rows and columns, like Heisenberg's frequencies. As Heisenberg had discovered, the multiplication of matrices is not commutative. With the help of Born and a second colleague, Pascual Jordan (1902–1980), Heisenberg reworked his early calculations, presenting the results in 1925.

↑ German-British physicist and mathematician Max Born introduced Heisenberg to the matrix.

Development of Quantum Mechanics

Using the matrix, it was possible to find a mathematical explanation of atomic structure. Heisenberg's model was fundamental to the development of quantum mechanics, or the laws determining the behavior of small-scale physical phenomena such as electrons and nuclei. Pauli's exclusion theory, developed by Wolfgang Pauli in 1925, was an important part of this new mechanic. It asserts that no two electrons in an atom can be in the same state or configuration at the same time.

Erwin Schrödinger, meanwhile, was formulating a different theory to describe the behavior of electrons in atoms based on French physicist Louis de Broglie's (1892–1987) proposal that particles in some situations act like waves. Schrödinger

Austrian-born Erwin Schrödinger formulated what became known as wave mechanics. In 1933, when this photograph was taken, he shared the Nobel Prize in Physics with another theoretical physicist, Paul Dirac.

described a "wave equation" with which he was able to predict broadly where, at any given point, the electron in the hydrogen atom might be found in relation to its nucleus. This approach to quantum mechanics became known as wave mechanics. For most people, imagining particles as waves was much easier than struggling with Heisenberg's obscure matrices, and Schrödinger's wave theory gained more general acceptance. Nevertheless, the importance of Heisenberg's matrix mechanics was recognized with the award of the 1932 Nobel Prize in Physics. Schrödinger shared it the following year with English theoretical physicist Paul Dirac. It was Dirac who showed that wave and matrix mechanics lead to the same answers.

Principle of Indeterminancy

Werner Heisenberg's name is most firmly linked with the "uncertainty principle," which he formulated in 1927. An alternative description is the "indeterminacy principle."

Heisenberg's principle states that the position and momentum of an object cannot both be measured exactly at the same time, even in theory. It is not something we notice in everyday life—it is obviously possible to know simultaneously the position and the velocity of an automobile, for example. This is because the uncertainties implied by the principle are far too small to be observed on the scale of ordinary objects. Only on the level of exceedingly small subatomic particles such as electrons, neutrons, or photons does the principle become significant. It is possible to know the position of an electron or to know its momentum, but not both at the same time. People often think that the uncertainty arises because instruments are too crude to measure a particle's position and its momentum at the same time, but the uncertainty principle in fact reflects the dual particle–wave nature of particles.

Heisenberg's uncertainty principle disturbed many scientists at the time, including Albert Einstein. It has been fiercely debated and analyzed ever since, yet the uncertainty principle has survived its critics and remains one of the fundamental planks of quantum mechanics.

Difficult Times

In 1933, the Nazi leader Adolf Hitler assumed power in Germany. Almost immediately, the purge of Jewish scientists from the country's universities and laboratories began. Many other scientists left Germany during the 1930s in protest against these acts, but Heisenberg chose to stay. Like Max Planck, who also stayed in Germany, Heisenberg was anxious to try and protect German scientific traditions and institutions. Although he was hostile to the policies of the Nazi regime, he did not openly oppose them. In 1941, Heisenberg was called to Berlin to take up a post as director of Kaiser Wilhelm Institute for Physics in Berlin.

After the war, Heisenberg returned to Göttingen. He wanted to restore and revive the reputation of German science. He founded and directed the Max Planck Institute for Physics for research in astrophysics and theoretical

Delegates attend the Copenhagen Conference of 1930 at the Institute for Theoretical Physics. Sitting in the front row, from left to right, are physicists Christian Klein, Niels Bohr, Werner Heisenberg, Wolfgang Pauli, George Gamow, Lev Landau, and Hendrik Kramers. Heisenberg first met Pauli when they were students together at the University of Munich, and they remained lifelong friends.

physics, which moved to Munich in 1948.

After Germany was defeated in 1945, the Allied occupying authorities banned German scientists from undertaking any further research into nuclear fission. Heisenberg worked hard to overturn this ban. He argued that the technology should be restricted to the production of nuclear energy, not for use as nuclear weaponry. When, partly through the efforts of Bohr, CERN was established in 1952, Heisenberg was appointed to head its scientific policy committee. He also continued his work on quantum theory and elementary particles until his retirement in 1970. He died in Munich on February 1, 1976.

Periodic Table of Elements

The periodic table organizes all the chemical elements into a simple chart according to the physical and chemical properties of their atoms. The elements are arranged by atomic number from 1 to 118. The atomic number is based on the number of protons in the nucleus of the atom. The atomic mass is the combined mass of protons and neutrons

KEY

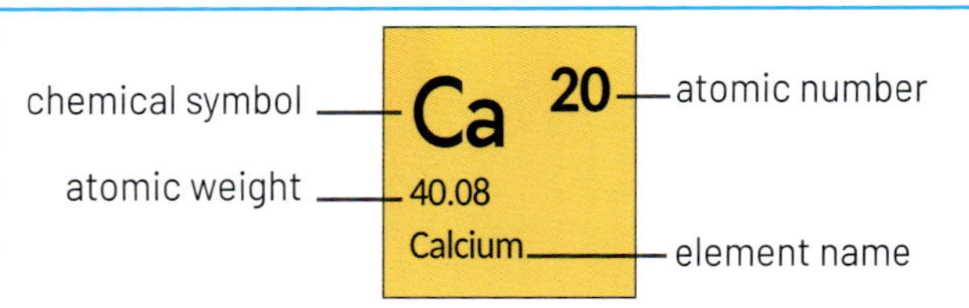

IA	IIA	IIIB	IVB	VB	VIB	VIIB	VIIIB1	VIIIB2	
H 1 1.008 Hydrogen									
Li 3 6.941 Lithium	Be 4 9.012 Beryllium								
Na 11 22.99 Sodium	Mg 12 24.31 Magnesium								
K 19 39.10 Potassium	Ca 20 40.08 Calcium	Sc 21 44.96 Scandium	Ti 22 47.87 Titanium	V 23 50.94 Vanadium	Cr 24 52 Chromium	Mn 25 54.94 Manganese	Fe 26 55.85 Iron	Co 27 58.93 Cobalt	58. Nic
Rb 37 85.47 Rubidium	Sr 38 87.62 Strontium	Y 39 88.91 Yttrium	Zr 40 91.22 Zirconium	Nb 41 92.91 Niobium	Mo 42 95.96 Molybdenum	Tc 43 [98] Technetium	Ru 44 101.1 Ruthenium	Rh 45 102.9 Rhodium	P 106 Pal
Cs 55 132.9 Caesium	Ba 56 137.3 Barium	5-71 La-lu Lanthanoids	Hf 72 178.5 Hafnium	Ta 73 180.9 Tantalum	W 74 183.8 Tungsten	Re 75 186.2 Rhenium	Os 76 190.2 Osmium	Ir 77 192.2 Iridium	P 195 Pla
Fr 87 [223] Francium	Ra 88 [226] Radium	89-103 Ac-Lr Actinoids	Rf 104 [265] Rutherfordium	Db 105 [268] Dubnium	Sg 106 [266] Seaborgium	Bh 107 [264] Bohrium	Hs 108 [277] Hassium	Mt 109 [276] Meitnerium	D [28 Dar

La 57 138.9 Lanthanum	Ce 58 140.1 Cerium	Pr 59 140.9 Praseodymium	Nd 60 144.2 Neodymium	Pm 61 [145] Promethium	Sm 62 150.4 Samarium	E 152 Eur
Ac 89 [227] Actinium	Th 90 232 Thorium	Pa 91 231 Protactinium	U 92 238 Uranium	Np 93 [237] Neptunium	Pu 94 [244] Plutonium	A [24 Am

in the nucleus. Each element has a chemical symbol that is an abbreviation of its name. In some cases, such as potassium, the symbol is an abbreviation of its Latin name ("K" stands for kalium). The name by which the element is commonly known is given in full underneath the symbol. The last item in the element box is the atomic mass. This is the average mass of an atom of the element.

Scientists have arranged the elements into vertical columns called groups and horizontal rows called periods. Elements in any one group have the same number of electrons in their outer shell and have similar chemical properties. Periods represent the increasing number of electrons it takes to fill the inner and outer shells and become stable. When all the spaces have been filled (Group 18 atoms have all their shells filled), the next period begins.

IB	IIB	IIIA	IVA	VA	VIA	VIIA	VIIIA
							He 2 4.003 Helium
		B 5 10.81 Boron	C 6 12.01 Carbon	N 7 14.01 Nitrogen	O 8 16.00 Oxygen	F 9 19.00 Fluorine	Ne 10 20.18 Neon
		Al 13 26.98 Aluminium	Si 14 28.09 Silicon	P 15 30.97 Phosphorus	S 16 32.06 Sulfur	Cl 17 35.45 Chlorine	Ar 18 39.95 Argon
29 er	Zn 30 65.38 Zinc	Ga 31 69.72 Gallium	Ge 32 72.63 Germanium	As 33 74.92 Arsenic	Se 34 78.96 Selenium	Br 35 79.90 Bromine	Kr 36 83.80 Krypton
g 47	Cd 48 112.4 Cadmium	In 49 114.8 Indium	Sn 50 118.71 Tin	Sb 51 121.76 Antimony	Te 52 127.6 Tellurium	I 53 126.9 Iodine	Xe 54 131.3 Xenon
u 79	Hg 80 200.6 Mercury	Tl 81 204.4 Thallium	Pb 82 207.2 Lead	Bi 83 209 Bismuth	Po 84 [209] Polonium	At 85 [210] Astatine	Rn 86 [222] Radon
111 genium	Cn 112 [285] Copernicium	Nh 113 [286] Nihonium	Fl 114 [289] Flerovium	Mc 115 [289] Moscovium	Lv 116 [293] Livermorium	Ts 117 [294] Tennessine	Og 118 [294] Oganesson
d 64 inium	Tb 65 158.9 Terbium	Dy 66 162.5 Dysprosium	Ho 67 164.9 Holmium	Er 68 167.3 Erbium	Tm 69 168.9 Thulium	Yb 70 173 Ytterbium	Lu 71 175 Lutetium
n 96 n	Bk 97 [247] Berkelium	Cf 98 [251] Californium	Es 99 [252] Einsteinium	Fm 100 [257] Fermium	Md 101 [258] Mendelevium	No 102 [259] Nobelium	Lr 103 [262] Lawrencium

- Alkali metals
- Alkali earth metals
- Noble gases
- Halogens
- Transition metals
- Lanthanoids
- Actinoids
- Metalloids
- Post transition metals
- Nonmetals

SCIENTIFIC BACKGROUND

Before 1910

English scientist John Dalton (1766–1844) devises his theory of the atom as a tiny solid particle.

German physicist Max Planck (1858–1947) suggests that light is emitted in separate packets called "quanta," or photons.

1910

1911 British physicist Ernest Rutherford (1871–1937) discovers that atoms have nuclei.

1913 Bohr proposes a new model of the atom.

1913 English radiochemist Frederick Soddy (1877–1956) introduces the word *isotope* to describe forms of the same element with different atomic weights.

1920

1922 Bohr is awarded the Nobel Prize for physics.

1924 French physicist Louis de Broglie (1892–1987) establishes the wave nature of electrons.

1927 Heisenberg proposes his uncertainty principle.

1930

1932 English physicist James Chadwick (1891–1974) discovers the neutron.

1932 Heisenberg is awarded the Nobel Prize for physics.

1940

1940 German-born scientists Otto Frisch (1904–1979) and Rudolf Peierls (1907–1995) calculate that it would only take a pound or two of uranium–235 to build an atomic bomb.

1943 Bohr begins work on the Manhattan Project at Los Alamos, New Mexico.

1950

1952 Heisenberg becomes head of the scientific policy committee of the European Council for Nuclear Research (CERN).

1960

1962 Bohr dies on November 18.

1964 American theoretical physicist Murray Gell-Mann (1929–2019) proposes that quarks are the fundamental building blocks of matter.

1965 American physicists Richard Feynman (1918–1988) and Julian Schwinger (1918–1994), and Japanese physicist Sin-Itiro Tomonaga (1906–1979), receive the Nobel Prize for physics for their work on quantum electrodynamics.

1970

1976 Heisenberg dies on February 2.

1980

After 1980

1986 Individual quantum jumps in individual atoms are observed.

1995 Particle physicists in Illinois identify the last of the six "flavors" of quarks, the elementary particles predicted by Gell-Mann in 1964; the six are known as: up, down, strange, charmed, bottom, and top.

POLITICAL AND CULTURAL BACKGROUND

1905 The Irish Nationalist Party, Sinn Féin (meaning "Ourselves Alone") is founded in Dublin as a means of mounting passive resistance to British rule.

1910

1915 A secret treaty between the Allies and Italy brings Italy into World War I (1914–18) on the Allied side.

1920

1922 The first issue of the monthly magazine *Reader's Digest* is published in the United States; it will become the world's biggest-selling magazine.

1930

1933 In Germany, the Nazis launch a campaign of persecution against the Jews, closing down Jewish-owned shops and ousting Jewish professors from universities.

1939 The invasion of Poland by Germany on September 1 marks the beginning of World War II (1939–45).

1940

1943 *Casablanca*, a wartime romance starring Humphrey Bogart (1899–1957) and Ingrid Bergman (1915–1982), wins the Academy Award for best motion picture.

1950

1962 The Cuban missile crisis erupts as the United States blockades Cuba to prevent the installation of Soviet missiles there.

1960

1976 *All the President's Men*, a film starring Dustin Hoffman (1937–) and Robert Redford (1937–), dramatizes the events surrounding the 1972 Watergate scandal.

1970

1978 In the United States, President Jimmy Carter (1924–) hosts talks between the leaders of Egypt and Israel at Camp David; a framework treaty is signed, ending 30 years of hostility between the two countries.

1980

Glossary

acid A substance that dissolves in water to form hydrogen ions (H^+). Acids are neutralized by bases and alkalis and have a pH below 7.

alchemist A person who attempted to change one substance into another using a combination of primitive chemistry and magic.

alpha particle The nucleus of a helium atom. This particle has two protons and two neutrons.

amorphous Describes something that lacks a defined structure or shape.

atom The smallest independent building block of matter. All substances are made of atoms.

atomic mass number The number of protons and neutrons in an atom's nucleus.

atomic number The number of protons in a nucleus.

Avogadro's number The number of atoms, molecules, or ions in one mole of a pure substance. This number is 602,21 3,670,000,000,000,000,000, or 6.0221367 x 10^{23}.

beta particle An electron emitted by a decaying radioactive element.

boiling point The temperature at which a liquid turns into a gas.

bond A chemical connection between atoms.

carbon dating Method for determining the age of a sample containing carbon.

chemical equation Symbols and numbers that show how reactants change into products during a chemical reaction.

chemical formula The letters and numbers that represent a chemical compound, such as "H_2O" for water.

chemical reaction The reaction of two or more chemicals (the reactants) to form new chemicals (the products).

chemical symbol The letters that represent a chemical, such as "Cl" for chlorine or "Na" for sodium.

compound A substance made from more than one element which has undergone a chemical reaction.

condensation The change of state from a gas to a liquid.

conductor A substance that carries electricity and heat.

covalent bond A bond in which atoms share electrons.

crystal A solid made of regular repeating patterns of atoms.

decay chain The sequence in which a radioactive element breaks down.

density The mass of substance in a unit of volume.

dipole attraction The attractive force between the electrically charged ends of molecules.

dissolve To form a solution.

distillation The process of evaporation and condensation used to separate a mixture of liquids according to their boiling points. Also a method of purifying a liquid.

electricity A stream of electrons or other charged particles moving through a substance.

electromagnetic radiation The energy emitted by a source such as X-rays, ultraviolet light, visible light, heat, or radio waves.

electromagnetic spectrum The range of energy waves that includes light, heat, and radio waves.

electron A tiny, negatively charged particle that moves around the nucleus of an atom.

electronegativity The power of an atom to attract an electron. Nonmetals, which have only a few spaces to fill in their outer shell, are the most electronegative elements. Metals, which have several empty spaces in their outer shells, tend to lose electrons in chemical reactions. Metals of this type are termed electropositive.

element A material that cannot be broken up into simpler ingredients. Elements contain only one type of atom.

energy The ability to do work.

energy level The shells around an atomic nucleus each represent a different energy level. Those closest to the nucleus have the lowest energy.

evaporation The change of state from a liquid to a gas when the liquid is at a temperature below its boiling point.

fission The process in which a large atom breaks up into two or more smaller fragments.

four elements The ancient theory that all matter consisted of only four "elements" (earth, air, fire, and water) and their combinations.

fusion The process by which two or more small atoms fuse to make a single larger atom.

gas The state in which particles are not joined and are free to move in any direction.

heterogeneous mixture A mixture in which different substances are spread unevenly throughout.

homogeneous mixture A mixture in which one substance has dissolved or been completely mixed into another.

hydrogen bond A weak dipole attraction that always involves a hydrogen atom.

intermolecular bond The bond that holds molecules together. These bonds are weaker than those between atoms in a molecule.

internal energy The total kinetic energy of all the particles in a system, plus all the chemical energy.

intramolecular bond Strong bond between atoms in a molecule.

ion An atom that has lost or gained one or more electrons and gained an electric charge.

ionic bond The attraction between positive and negative ions in an ionic compound.

ionization The formation of ions by adding or removing electrons from atoms.

isotope Any atoms of a given element must have the same number of protons but can have different numbers of neutrons. These different versions of the same element are called isotopes.

law of conservation of mass The law that states that in a chemical reaction, the total mass of the products is always equal to the total mass of the reactants.

liquid A substance in which particles are loosely bonded and are able to move freely around each other.

lubricant A substance that helps surfaces slide past each other.

malleable Describes a material that can be hammered into different shapes without breaking. Metals are malleable.

matter Anything that can be weighed.

melting point The temperature at which a solid changes into a liquid. When a liquid changes into a solid, this same temperature is also called the freezing point.

metal An element that is solid, shiny, malleable, ductile, and conductive.

metallic bond The bond in which outer electrons are free to move in the spaces between the atoms.

mixture Matter made from different types of substances that are not physically or chemically bonded together.

mole The amount of any substance that contains the same number of atoms as in 12 grams of carbon-12 atoms. This number is 6.022×10^{23}.

molecule Two or more bonded atoms that form a substance with specific properties.

neutron One of the particles that makes up the nucleus of an atom. Neutrons do not have any electric charge.

noble gases A group of gases that rarely react with other elements.

nonmetal Any element that is not a metal. Most nonmetals are gases, such as hydrogen and argon.

nucleus The central part of an atom. The nucleus contains protons and neutrons. The exception is hydrogen, which contains only one proton.

particle The smallest portion or amount of something.

photon A particle that carries a quantity of energy, such as in the form of light.

plasma The "fourth state of matter" in which atoms have lost some or all of their electrons.

plastic An organic polymer that can be molded or shaped into objects or films by heat.

pressure The force produced by pressing on something.

product A new substance or substances created by a chemical reaction.

proton A positively charged particle found in an atom's nucleus.

radiation The products of radioactivity—alpha and beta particles and gamma rays.

radioactive decay The breakdown of an unstable nucleus through the loss of alpha and beta particles.

reactant The ingredient necessary for a chemical reaction.

relative atomic mass A measure of the mass of an atom compared with the mass of another atom. The values used are the same as those for atomic mass.

relative molecular mass The sum of all the atomic masses of the atoms in a molecule.

salt A compound made from positive and negative ions that forms when an alkali reacts with an acid.

shell The orbit of an electron. Each shell can contain a specific number of electrons and no more.

solid The state of matter in which particles are held in a rigid arrangement.

state The form that matter takes—either a solid, a liquid, or a gas.

subatomic particles Particles that are smaller than an atom.

supernova The explosion of a very large star.

temperature A measure of how fast molecules are moving. It indicates the heat being given off by something.

valence electrons The electrons in the outer shell of an atom.

van der Waals forces Short-lived forces between atoms and molecules.

volume The space that a solid, liquid, or gas occupies.

Further Information

American Chemical Society (ACS)
1155 Sixteenth Street NW
Washington, DC 20036
(800) 333-9591
Website: portal.acs.org
The ACS represents professionals in all fields of chemistry. Its Division of Organic Chemistry (**www.organicdivision.org**) specifically promotes the advancement of the field of organic chemistry.

Chemical Institute of Canada
222 Queen Street, Suite 1009
Ottawa, Ontario
Canada K1P 5V9
(613) 232-6252
Website: www.cheminst.ca
This organization of chemists, chemical engineers, and chemical technologists works to advance the sciences in a range of areas, including health care, pharmaceuticals, energy, food, and water.

International Union of Pure and Applied Chemistry (IUPAC)
P.O. Box 13757
Research Triangle Park, NC 27709-3757
(919) 485-8700
Website: www.iupac.org
The IUPAC advances the chemical sciences by fostering worldwide communication and education in the chemical sciences. It is the world authority on chemical nomenclature and standardized measurement methods.

Jefferson Lab
12000 Jefferson Avenue
Newport News, VA 23606
(757) 269-7100
Website: www.jlab.org
Jefferson Lab studies the atomic nucleus and performs applied research with industries and universities. It also offers science education programs for people of all ages.

National Academy of Sciences
The Keck Center
500 Fifth Street NW
Washington, DC 20001
(202) 334-2000
Website: www.nasonline.org
This society provides objective guidance to people in the fields of science and technology. Its website offers the latest news on current academic research and government policy.

National Science Foundation (NSF)
2415 Eisenhower Avenue
Alexandria, VA 22314
(703) 292-5111
Website: www.nsf.gov
This U.S. agency promotes education and research in the sciences and engineering. Its website includes updates on chemistry and materials discoveries.

TRIUMF
4004 Westbrook Mall
Vancouver, BC V6T 2A3
Canada
(604) 222-1047
Website: www.triumf.ca
TRIUMF is a renowned Canadian subatomic physics laboratory that also offers high school education and outreach programs to promote science and research.

Science History Institute
315 Chestnut Street
Philadelphia, PA 19106
(215) 925-2222
Website: sciencehistory.org/visit/exhibitions
Formed by the merger of the Chemical Heritage Foundation and the Life Sciences Foundation, the Institute's museum features a permanent exhibition that explains how chemistry has influenced people, along with other changing exhibits on a variety of subjects.

Youth Science Canada
P.O. Box 297
Pickering, ON L1V 2R4
Canada
(866) 341-0040
Website: www.youthscience.ca
This organization encourages young people to participate in project-based science by making programs available to them. Youth Science Canada holds the Canada-Wide Science Fair every year to celebrate young scientists and their experiments.

Books

Ball, Philip, Zhu, Wenting and Liang, Yan. *The Beauty of Chemistry: Art, Wonder and Science*. Cambridge, MA: MIT Press, 2021.

Berk Koch, Susan and Rauch, Micah. *Chemical Reactions!* Norwich, VT: Nomad Press, 2021.

Berners-Lee, Mike. *The Carbon Footprint of Everything.* London, UK: Greystone Books, 2022.

Challoner, Jack. *The Atom: A Visual Tour.* Cambridge, MA: MIT Press, 2018.

Congdon, Lisa. *The Illustrated Encyclopedia of the Elements: The Powers, Uses and Histories of Every Atom in the Universe.* San Francicsco, CA: Chronicle Books, 2021.

Dorling Kindersley. *The Chemistry Book.* London, UK: Dorling Kindersley, 2022.

Gray, Theodore and Mann, Nick. *Molecules: The Elements and the Architecture of Everything.* New York, NY: Black Dog and Leventhal, 2018.

Hazen, Robert M. *Symphony in C: Carbon and the Evolution of (Almost) Everything.* VCVCV Norton, 2019.

Jolpic Science! *Atomic Theory for Kids.* New York, NY: Jolpic Science, 2022.

Klein, David R. *Organic Chemistry as a Second Language.* Hoboken, NJ: Wiley, 2019.

Linde, Barbara Martina. *Atoms: It Matters.* New York, NY: Rosen Publishing, 2020.

Lowe, Derek B. *The Chemistry Book: From Gunpowder to Graphene, 250 Milestones in the History of Chemistry.* New York, NY: Union Square and Co, 2022.

Moore, John T. *Chemistry Essentials for Dummies.* London, UK: For Dummies, 2019.

Morris Parker, Bertha. *Matter, Molecules and Atoms.* New York, NY: Yesterday's Classics, 2018.

NEDU. *Chemistry Made Easy: An Illustrated Study Guide for Students To Easily Learn Chemistry.* Cheyenne, WY: NEDU LLC, 2021.

Nguyen-Kim, Mai Thi and Lenkova, Claire. *Chemistry for Breakfast.* London, UK: Greystone Books, 2022.

Post, Richard et al. *Chemistry: Concepts and Problems, A Self Teaching Guide.* Hoboken, NJ: John Wiley, 2020.

Scientific American. *Ask the Experts: Chemistry.* New York, NY: Rosen Publishing, 2018.

Sezer, Ali O. *Chemistry: An Illustrated Guide for All Ages.* New York, NY: Barron's, 2021.

Smithsonian. *The Elements Book: A Visual Encyclopedia of the Periodic Table.* New York, NY: Dorling Kindersley, 2017.

Sterling Education. *High School Chemistry: Comprehensive Content for High-School Chemistry.* New York, NY: Sterling Education, 2022.

Index

D

E

F

G

H

I

R

S

T

U

V

W

X

Photo Credits

Front Cover: iStock: vchal.

DeAgostini Picture Library: CHOMON 37t ; **Getty Images:** Bloomberg 13, Keystone France/Gamma Keystone 70, Keystone/Hulton Archive 75, Photoresearchers/Charles Falco 62, Photoresearchers/Charles D Winters 18, 43, UIG 15, 24, 30, 44, 46t, 56, 59, 64; **Imagno:** Austrian Archives 20t; **iStock:** soubrette 26, Thinkstock 12, 60, Alexey Ukhov 48; **Library of Congress:** 39; **Photos.com:** 72; **Public Domain:** 76; **Science & Society Picture Library:** 20b, 23b, 77, Science Museum 79; **Science Source:** Drs Ali Yasdani & Daniel j. Homba 22, Gusto 67, James King Holmes 32; **Shutterstock:** ancoay 28, Michal Balada 55, Catarina Belova 14, Marty Benny 10, Marcel Clemesn 21, DDCoral 53, dugdax 40, Matej Hudovernick 46b, I am a Stranger 50, Yury Koroursov 52, KREML 58, Melanie Lemahieu 23t, HK Ling 6, Viacheslav Lopatin 51, Ivanko Lubo 34, muratart 3, 66, Anna Pustynnikova 17, Yaroslav Sabitov 7, simlinger 47, Simon's passion 4 travel 38, Smileus 42, Dani Sugandi 8.

All other photos and illustrations Brown Bear Books Ltd.

Brown Bear Books has made every attempt to contact the copyright holder.
Please email licensing@brownbearbooks.co.uk with any information about omissions.